INDUSTRIAL RELATIONS

Ken Whitehead worked as a clerk for thirteen years, during which time he became an active trade unionist, rising from shop steward to delegate to the national conference. He subsequently left his job to attend Ruskin College, Oxford, and York University, where he read History and Economics. He has since worked as a union research officer and has also served for a year on the Commission on Industrial Relations.

Ken Whitehead at present lectures in Industrial Relations and organizes courses for shop stewards at Harrow College of Technology.

TEACH YOURSELF BOOKS

INDUSTRIAL RELATIONS

Ken Whitehead

Editorial Adviser: Ronald Chappell
Dean of the Faculty of Social Sciences
Harrow College of Technology and Art

TEACH YOURSELF BOOKS
Hodder and Stoughton

First impression 1977
Third impression 1981

Copyright © 1977

Ken Whitehead

ISBN 0 340 220821

Printed and bound in Great Britain for
Hodder and Stoughton Paperbacks,
a division of Hodder and Stoughton Ltd,
Mill Road, Dunton Green, Sevenoaks, Kent
(Editorial Office, 47 Bedford Square, London WC1 3DP)
by Richard Clay (The Chaucer Press) Ltd,
Bungay, Suffolk

Contents

Part Two: Collective Bargaining and Participation

Introduction

This book aims to introduce the major themes of industrial relations and to show readers that this is a valid approach to the problems of industrial society. Taking the viewpoint of man at work and then looking at relevant institutions and conventions has the value of bringing together what might otherwise be disconnected studies: history, economics, sociology and so on. A good deal has to be borrowed (if that is the right word) from these separate disciplines, but their relevance to our immediate problems is made more apparent from the industrial relations viewpoint. Labour power comes from complete human beings with a total relationship to society; they are not just a factor of production nor even just trade unionists. Understanding their problems and aspirations gives an insight into the type of society we live in.

It might be possible to advance that argument as regards any form of society that we have ever known. Be that as it may, we did not talk about industrial relations before the industrial revolution. So far as this book is concerned we are dealing with a particular historical context and not with eternal laws. Our context is the long industrial revolution, which began in Britain about two hundred years ago and is still spreading throughout the world without any sign of abatement.

Industrialisation takes away from the worker control over his employment and interest in his work. Work becomes, to parody Lord Byron, a thing apart. Workers have reacted in a number of ways against this system which is tantamount to wage slavery: Luddites smashed machinery, Chartists threatened a violent revolution. Even today, industrial discontent may take a number of incipient forms such as absenteeism, poor workmanship, and sheer vandalism on occasions. Such expressions do not provide the same focus on problems of industrial relations as does trade unionism, and for this reason our subject concentrates heavily upon trade unions. It is not, however, simply about 'trade unions and that sort of thing'. It is about those relationships that are peculiar to man at work in the conditions of an industrial society. Other approaches may reveal a variety of causes that have nothing whatever to do with the industrialised nature of work. Absenteeism may be due to a 'flu epidemic, which is clearly outside the scope of our studies. A strike, on the other hand, is an overt expression of industrial discontent, and that is our concern.

Although trade unions provide the best window through which to study industrial relations, they are not the only relevant institution. The first section of this book, which describes the principal relevant institutions, also introduces employers' organisations and modern management. The state might also have been brought in at this stage, except that traditionally it is only supposed to be a third party to any industrial dispute, and it has a role which is too complex to understand without first knowing something about the realities of free collective bargaining.

Free collective bargaining is dealt with in a second section in which there is also a chapter on the role of government. Collective bargaining is the traditional way that trade unions seek to increase industrial democracy. There are other methods, including participation, and these are the subject of another chapter. As a whole, this section describes the various ways that the principal participants reconcile their differences.

A third section deals with the present critical stage of industrial relations in Britain, and looks at various possible remedies. The point has to be made that conventional industrial relations, dealings between employers and unions with occasional state intervention, are running more and more into contradictions. State intervention is not occasional but persistent and the future of free collective bargaining is in doubt. It seems that a more direct approach to the alienating nature of industrial work is necessary. A final chapter looks at some signposts for the future, including the exciting prospects opened up by the proponents of alternative technology.

After every chapter there is a note on further reading. The books selected should be fairly easy to obtain and easy to read. They are not intended to give students a select bibliography as this is easily obtained from more advanced texts. Nor is every choice to be found on the shelf marked 'Industrial Relations'. For example, my own first choice would be George Orwell's *Animal Farm*.

There are also questions for discussion, which are meant to be just that. Unless I have made a mistake none of them admits of a ready answer. Industrial relations is not the sort of subject to encourage dogmatism. Occasionally, the text has over-simplified a problem for teaching purposes, and questions at the end of the chapter have sought to remedy this.

Part One: The Principal Institutions

I

Why Trade Unions?

Why should there be trade unions at all? Why don't people stand on their own feet, to use a popular phrase? This chapter will attempt to answer that type of question. It will be seen that an industrial society creates a particular type of work with a distinct relationship between the worker and his employer. Within that context trade unions become essential. If they were suppressed, the whole industrial system would be subject to unbearable stresses and strains. The easiest way to show this is to trace the effects of the Industrial Revolution as it overtook British workers from the last quarter of the eighteenth century. If the writing moves on occasion from the past to the present tense, that is because the Industrial Revolution has never ended. The same processes, the same economic logic, the same way of looking at the meaning of life (or perhaps ignoring the question)—all of these things are still with us.

Although every aspect of industrial work will be mentioned, the reader should not form too gloomy a picture. Trade unions have not struggled in vain to defend their members' interests, and the progress of industrialisation is extremely patchy; as a result, different occupations have been affected in varying degrees. But unless we have a proper understanding of all the hopes and fears of workers we cannot understand the role of modern trade unions. It will be seen that they have come to work within the system, to change the relationships originally imposed or threatened.

There have been associations of workmen since medieval

times and some of their features are still to be found in unions of craftsmen. Those Journeymen's Guilds, however, answered different needs from those of a modern trade union, and the reasoning which lay behind them will not take us very far towards an understanding of their modern counterparts.

The industrial revolution began in Britain when the markets of the world were opened to her manufacturers. Previously most manufacture had been carried out in small workshops, which were quite suitable for a small market. A single blacksmith could well provide all the ironwork for his village. But when these articles could be sold in hundreds of thousands in a vast market, a new technology was called for. Instead of a single smithy, there developed factories or mills. each specialising in the production of one item. Adam Smith, the father of modern economics, noted that the first requisite of mass-production is the existence of a sufficiently large market. Historically, many other reasons are needed to explain why that revolution should have started just where and when it did, but the one especially relevant to our present concern is the availability of sufficient funds to finance these new mills and factories. Large sums were required for buildings, plant and machinery. Further capital investment was necessary to build the canals, roads and railways for the easy transport of goods around the country and to the ports.

Very few families were wealthy enough to finance enterprises on the scale, say, of a railway from Birmingham to London. A considerable number of people had to pool their resources in a joint-stock company. Prior to the introduction of *limited liability*, which means that an investor only stands to lose the sum he has subscribed, this could be a very hazardous business. Although an individual investor could have little control over an enterprise, he was liable to the full extent of his personal fortune. The legal invention of limited liability cleared the way for industrial capital to be organised. Subsequently Parliament was to perform a similar service for labour, but that story comes later.

The immediate effect of industrialisation upon workers

was that they were drawn together in greater numbers and at the same time put at a greater distance from their employers. The old craftsman had only to turn his head to voice a complaint or offer a suggestion to his master. Children who helped at home with spinning could tug at their mother's skirts. How could any of them talk to a joint-stock company? The owners of a company were now numbered by the thousand, scattered all over the country, and some of them would never so much as set eyes on the firm they partly owned, let alone actually talk to its employees. Nor do they today. For most of the nineteenth century there were important family firms which were managed in a paternalist style. Some of them even survived well into this century. That arrangement is now largely confined to small-scale business, and investors become increasingly remote from employees as their funds are managed by institutions —insurance companies, unit trusts, etc. Common sense dictates that it is better 'not to have all your eggs in one basket'. An individual investor tends to have his money spread over a wide range of firms so that his interest in any one of them is purely financial.

The problem is not just one of communications. Victorian critics of industrial society could see clearly the world they had lost. Instead of traditional bonds—honour, charity, good manners, social obligation, call them what you will—the only link between the two parties was a purely financial one. Labour itself had become another commodity to be bought and sold. A wide range of writers reviled what came to be called 'the cash nexus'. This estrangement of employers from workers is the first aspect of what is referred to as the *alienation* of industrial work, and this is à theme which will constantly recur.

Division of labour

One of the economies of large-scale production arises from 'division of labour'. This means that when there is a large workforce it is possible to divide and subdivide a job into a number of minute, repetitive tasks. Immediately, this dispenses with the need for relatively expensive skilled labour. Workers can be brought straight off the street to do a lot of the simple jobs which are left. People working at a repetitive task are able to build up a considerable speed and this makes the product still cheaper. Instead of moving around his workshop to pick up different tools and materials, an operative stays in one place and work is constantly fed to him.

There are further economies to be made when a task is so simplified that it is possible to use power-driven machinery. Suppose that a worker spends all day just sawing through planks of wood. His hand-saw can be replaced with a power-driven circular saw which will do the job much more quickly. Investment in that piece of machinery becomes worth while because it is in constant use. At first water-power was used a good deal, especially in textile industries on the slopes of the Pennines. Later coal was used to provide steam-power. The benefits of all this are obvious enough from the point of view of employers and their customers. Employers cut their costs, and customers get an abundance of cheap, mass-manufactured goods.

But from the workers' point of view, division of labour, when carried to an extreme, is very far from a blessing. Work becomes monotonous and boring. Once all skill has been taken out of work it is not possible to take any pride in it. Alienation of the worker from his work is not the end of the matter. Under conditions of mass manufacture, very few workers have any contact with their customers. On some modern production lines workers may not even know what it is that they are helping to make. There is no satisfaction in the actual job, no pride in the end-product and none of the personal satisfaction that comes from doing something for a person you can meet and talk to for a while. If you just contrast that village blacksmith mentioned earlier with a worker in the middle of a production line, the picture should become clear. When work has been so completely industrialised, the only motive left to a worker is the money that comes at the end of the week.

Work is further dehumanised by close supervision. Little trust can be placed in someone who simply does a job for money. Supervision is necessary to see that work is done properly. Even if these operatives are to be trusted, it is still necessary to co-ordinate all the minute tasks they perform. Every worker's output must fit into overall production plans for so many completed items. The larger a firm becomes, the longer become lines of communication. From supervisors or foremen actually watching workers, there arises a whole management hierarchy. All too often when orders finally reach workers, they appear to make little sense. Beside other forms of alienation we must set alienation from management.

As industry advances there is a tendency for capital equipment to become more and more expensive. Such equipment depreciates in value with time and it is important that it should not be left standing idle for any longer than is absolutely essential. Shifts are introduced including nightwork, so that against their nature some human beings become nocturnal creatures.

A constant drive to make the maximum use of labour, to improve productivity, has in this century caused the development of work-study techniques. Their effect is to dictate the precise *manner* in which work is performed. Seconds or fractions of seconds are saved by perhaps changing some precise movements of hands and feet. The very last vestige of personal responsibility may be thus removed.

Health and safety aspects of industrial work

In the nineteenth century, Britain's demand for coal meant that mines were driven farther and deeper underground. Consequently, mining became an ever-more dangerous occupation. Flooding, subsidence, and explosions of natural gas caused pit disasters. Coal dust gave miners a special lung disease which killed even more. Girls working in match factories developed a horrible disease called 'phosphur jaw'. Power-driven machinery always tends to be more dangerous and is more so when, as in the nineteenth century, it was minded by young children tired out from working twelve hours a day.

We no longer have children working in factories, and most machinery must be adequately fenced by law. We know about the dangers of working with phosphorous substances, and that particular disease has been eliminated. Mining conditions have improved but we have not got rid of 'miner's disease'. New products and processes may bring in fresh hazards. At the time of writing, newspapers are covering a report into the deaths of men working in an asbestos plant. Trade unions, in fact, are becoming increasingly alarmed about the 'invisible' hazards of noise, fumes and dust.

Economic insecurity

Many skilled workers have always owned their own tools. These craftsmen have a certain amount of independence. In previous centuries, when work became scarce or just intolerable for some reason, a craftsman would simply pack his tools and set off round the country to find some other employment. The trade society in each town that he visited would help him to find work. That system was known as 'tramping'. Today we do not find so many independent craftsmen and they certainly do not go tramping around the country. We use the word 'tramp' to describe quite a different type of person. Some craft unions still refer to a qualified craftsman as a 'journeyman' but that seems to be the last trace of tramping. The majority of workers do not own their own tools; it is not possible in an age of massive capital investment. In order to earn their living they must use employers' equipment.

In addition to alienation from the means of production, there is the point that division of labour tends to deprive the worker of special skills which are saleable to the general public. A carpenter may find some work from his neighbours, but only another mass-manufacturer will require the minute skill of a worker off the assembly line. Highly specialised workers can only sell their skills to mass-production employers, and are therefore bound to work for wages.

Wages are usually paid for a fairly short period of time; a week is most common. Before the days of the welfare state, workers were soon in dire economic straits if they lost their jobs. States now provide a greater degree of economic security. Nevertheless, the working class is marked by a sense of insecurity. Before being caught by the state's safety net, they usually suffer a considerable fall in living standards. They do not commonly possess sufficient savings for it to be otherwise, nor do they have assets on which they can be advanced a great deal of credit. There is a marked contrast in this respect with the middle classes, who tend to feel more secure, and on that account to show more initiative. Where that sense of security has been lessened, in industrial management for example, these people are turning to trade unionism.

It is difficult for us to appreciate the resentment of early industrial workers against the wage system. We have never known anything else and so, it seems, one might as well criticise the moon and the stars. They knew hard work, poverty, and even starvation and conditions such as these drove many from the land to find work in industry. However, they were not accustomed to the sheer inhumanity and degradation of industrial life. Their smallholdings had given them some measure of independence, however hard life might be. When people from the countryside brought their habit of keeping pigs or chickens into a town like Manchester, they only increased the squalor. Industrial towns provided barrack-like accommodation for their armies of workers without even the smallest of gardens. Many families lived in cellars. For traditional craftsmen the situation was even worse, as they did not even see more money. Migrant workers, particularly from Ireland, depressed their material living standards as wages were driven down to the subsistence level of the poorest of peasants. Whether better fed or not, workers under the new system were totally dependent upon wages and came to refer to industrial capitalism as 'wage slavery'. Arguments about whether material living standards were higher or lower for the majority of the working class are nothing to the main point of alienation. After all there can be such a thing as a well-fed slave.

Political and industrial democracy

The question for workers was what to do about it. Trade unions as we now know them have only evolved very gradually. First reactions were violent in some parts of the country. Groups called Luddites went round with sledge-hammers smashing the new machinery; mill-owners were defended by the military or their own private armies, and their encounters with Luddites resembled pitched battles on occasion, with dead left on both sides.

During the second quarter of the nineteenth century a variety of more sophisticated though not always less violent movements arose. Labour appeared to twist this way and that in its endeavours to be rid of industrial capitalism. General trade unions had a short revolutionary phase but exhausted themselves financially with premature confrontations. Chartists chose the political road. From 1838 to 1848 they strove to obtain political rights for the working classes, thinking that once they had power they could right all the wrongs of industrialisation. There were serious riots, particularly in 1842, and many Chartists were sent to prison. That movement was defeated and Land Chartism followed; groups of workers bought land to develop as smallholdings. Some of their villages are still to be seen, and the movement gave birth to a well-known British building society. Throughout the nineteenth century there were attempts to set up 'producer co-operatives', self-governing workshops, from a variety of motives. They nearly all failed. The reasons for their failure will be discussed in more detail in the chapter on participation, but generally they were out of keeping with their time.

The second half of the nineteenth century saw a marked shift away from revolutionary ventures. Compelled to accept industrial capitalism without any measure of political democracy, workers gradually formed a sort of permanent opposition within industry—the modern trade union movement. Early in this century there was one further up-surge of revolutionary trade unionism bent upon over-throwing the whole system. But in the main, trade unions have been collective bargainers with reformist politics as a second activity.

The logic of trade unions is not hard to see. Clearly the individual worker was and is in a hopeless position as against the economic power of a large company. A reasonable bargain is only likely to be struck if both sides are of about the same weight. A large company may manage indefinitely without the services of an individual worker, whereas he or she is compelled to find some employment in order to live decently.

But if these large groups of workers stand together they can match the power of their employer. One worker can be ignored, but the entire work-force cannot. Mass-production in fact laid the essential foundations of collective bargaining. Working together in large groups, it was easy for workers to see their common interests and act together. Division of labour made their work co-operative; each worker contributed a small part to the final product. Under these conditions nothing was more natural than that they should adopt a collectivist approach. An element of danger, as in mining, makes for uniformity, since a man's life may depend upon a close understanding within the working group. Modern trade unions are the children of industrialisation. Employers for their part have found that they can co-exist with collective bargainers.

The consequences of this historical development are still very much with us and it will pay to dwell on them. At the heart of the matter is the trade unions' decision to work within the existing system. From that arises some confusion about the role or objectives of unions in our type of society. One school of thought has it that unions exist merely to make the system work, that they are a safety valve to release discontent without endangering any basic relationships. At the other extreme is a view of unions as being quite incompatible with industrial capitalism. They are, on this account, an objectionable nuisance and society would be better off without them. This argument finds support in the fact that it is difficult if not impossible to show statistically that trade unions have lifted wages above the level they would have reached in any case. It seems to follow that at best they are futile and at worst a positive hindrance to industrial progress. Both versions express a kind of half-truth and fail to appreciate the very real contribution which unions have made to both industrial and political democracy.

As a matter of historical fact, the immediate political aims of Chartism were dropped in favour of an industrial approach. The modern trade union movement does not offer any clear alternative to capitalism. Trade unions are essentially organisations of employees concerned with getting better wages and conditions from existing employers. They do not bend their efforts to the destruction of those employers. Most union officials will cheerfully admit that they like to see high profits because that makes it easier for them to get better wages and conditions. All of that supports the 'safety valve' argument. Sometimes this is expressed as a theory of countervailing power: organised labour provides a check or balance to the power of organised capital.

But to appreciate the range of trade union activity we must remember the extent of alienation associated with industrial work. Unions have striven with some success to give workers a degree of control over their working lives. With collective bargaining as their main weapon, they have largely destroyed the tyranny of Victorian employers and substituted 'joint control', that is, control by unions and employers working together on a wide range of issues. Anyone who doubts this must read more about the great industrial struggles of labour history.

A modern collective agreement does not just deal with wages but with a wide variety of topics which were once decided entirely by management acting in the interests of employers. The history of industrial relations might almost be written as a struggle over managerial prerogatives.

Manning levels, recruitment, dismissals, working rules, safety regulations, training, promotions, and many other items may all be subject to joint control. Agreement has to be reached between the two parties before a rule is established. There is room for argument amongst economists as to whether unions have much effect on the level of wages; but there is no doubt as to their effectiveness in extending industrial democracy.

An industrial *approach* does not have to stop when it meets a political barrier. This story will be told in more detail in subsequent chapters; but, very briefly, unions were forced into the political arena in order to continue to exist and subsequently created the Labour Party because some of their objectives could not be obtained without the backing of Parliament. There is no clear line to be drawn between industrial and political democracy. A mass of legislation applies to workplaces, much of it instigated by trade unions. Less specific but just as important to unions, are economic and social policies of government which may improve the lot of the working class generally. Trade unionism does not stop at the factory gate.

At the same time it would be wrong to extend our argument to the point where we saw each trade union as holding itself responsible for the welfare of the whole working class. First and foremost a union is concerned with the interests of its own members. It is quite possible for a union's policy to run contrary to that of another or even appear to be against 'national interests'. Unions become annoyed when criticised for not having sufficient regard for outsiders. As the TUC said in its evidence to the Donovan Commission, the same could be said of any firm. A company seeks to maximise its profits as a prime objective, a union seeks to improve its members' wages and conditions as a prime objective. Neither organisation expects this order of priorities to be cited as proof that their existence is not in the common interest. Unions have never pretended to be all things to all men. They simply claim the same right as other associations in a free society, which is to pursue their members' interests.

There has to be some control of all self-interested groups—
or any other association for that matter—but that is quite
a different question from their right to look after themselves.

FURTHER READING

The First Principles of Industrial Relations by A. E. C. Hare
(Macmillan, 2nd ed. 1965) has a very clear analysis of
the nature of industrial work.

Animal Farm by George Orwell (Longmans 1960) is essential reading. Written in a very simple style as if for
children, it is in fact a brilliant satire on any society that
makes a god of production, be it capitalist or socialist.

Some grasp of the history of the labour movement is necessary, because so much has been historically determined.
G. D. H. Cole's *A Short History of the British Working Class
Movement* (Allen and Unwin 1948) is a very useful book
for students of trade unions. Henry Pelling's *A History of
British Trade Unionism* (Macmillan, 2nd. Ed. 1972) is another useful book. Finally, one must mention *The Common
People* by G. D. H. Cole and Raymond Postgate (Methuen
1961) which is a classic and gives an overall view of
working class history.

QUESTIONS FOR DISCUSSION

1 What is missing from the motto 'A fair day's work for
a fair day's pay'?
2 How would you describe the working class?
3 Are students' unions in any way comparable to trade
unions?

Why So Many Trade Unions?

We have yet to appreciate the need for more than one trade union. All members of an industrial society must be affected by the type of society they live in. But they are not all affected in the same way or to anything like the same degree. Some employees still see no good reason for joining any union at all. At any one time only about half of Britain's workforce is unionised, although of the remainder some are having a 'free ride' (accepting benefits without paying contributions), and others may be in a union at odd times. Of those in unions there will be differences of interest according to the manner or degree that they are affected by industrialisation.

It would be quite wrong, however, to create the impression that technology is all that there is to consider. Historical, geographical, even cultural factors all play their part. When we come in another chapter to look at unions in Europe as a whole we shall have to take into account religion and political ideology. There is no limit on factors which can destroy that unity of interests which one union demands.

In Britain it is possible to see four main types of union: craft, general, industrial and white collar, although this last is a very mixed bag. Taking each type in turn will serve to show at least major differences of interest, and their causes.

Craft unions

Craft unions, strictly speaking, are exclusively for skilled men. Originally there was one union for one trade. Hence the name 'trade union' instead of 'trades union'. Nowadays 'trade union' is the term applied, however inaccurately, to all types of union, even in Acts of Parliament. Craft unions themselves now usually cover more than one trade owing to amalgamations and changes in working methods. In addition there are some craft unions which are now open to unskilled workers but which remain dominated by craftsmen.

Pre-industrial craft societies sought to restrict the supply of a particular skill. The saying was 'When eggs are scarce eggs are dear, when men are scarce men are dear'. Scarcity was maintained in a number of ways. Only society members were allowed to do certain types of work. If a 'foreigner', meaning someone who was not a society member, came into the workshop, other workmen would do their best to drive him out. And their best was usually good enough. There were restrictions on the number of apprentices allowed to each journeyman. Secrets of the trade were jealously guarded. Elaborate initiation ceremonies were calculated to make a lasting impression on new entrants and instill in them the belief that they must never reveal a trade secret. These societies were organised locally rather than nationally. Many of them acted as friendly societies providing benefits for members who suffered some misfortune.

'New Model Unionism'

Modern trade unionism is usually dated from 1851 when the Amalgamated Society of Engineers (ASE) was formed by pulling together local craft societies in engineering. Similar developments occured in other trades. The Amalgamated Society of Carpenters, for example, was formed in 1861, closely modelled on the ASE. Besides being national organisations, there were other changes which can best be appreciated by recollecting their historical context.

Revolutionary unions of the 1830s had suffered ignominious defeat, partly from being too hasty to confront employers. 'New Model Unions' were to be much more prudent, keen in fact to avoid strikes by conciliation and arbitration whenever possible. Chartism had also been defeated in its attempt to form an independent political organisation. 'New Model Unions' hitched their wagon to the Liberal Party. Some of their leaders were in the pay of that party's chief whip.

Chartism and those early general unions recruited from all the working classes. The expression 'working classes' rather than 'working class' (singular) is correct in this period, because craftsmen formed a separate social class. It was these craftsmen, often referred to as 'the labour aristocracy', who in the 1850s and 60s remodelled their old craft societies in order to cope with the industrial revolution. Defeated in their attempts to secure control in combination with other working people, they were to see whether on their own they could come to some sort of agreement with employers. New Model Unions presented a highly respectable front to the world. They abandoned the image of small secret societies, and became instead national organisations with printed rule books and full-time officials. These rules contained little if anything to upset the established order. References to producer co-operatives were fairly harmless, and never took up much of their energies. They retained the same restrictive practices, but, far from being revolutionary, on the whole these could be said to be hallowed by ancient custom and practice. However, it is also true that some of the most bitter disputes of the nineteenth century were fought over this question of who should control workshop practice.

Craft unions of today are the successors of those New Model Unions. Although the Electrical Trade Union was not formed until a much later date, it too was modelled on the ASE. The ASE itself has evolved into the AUEW and is one of those craft unions which now accept unskilled members and yet remain dominated by a craft outlook.

The craft mentality

The work which craftsmen do is not nearly so alienated as that described in the first chapter. Their ideal view of themselves might be taken from the trade magazine *Machinery* in 1915:

> '... He is engaged in tasks where the capacity for original thought is exercised; he has refined and critical perception of the things pertaining to his craft. His work creates a feeling of self-reliance ... he lives a full and satisfying life; neither hypocrisy nor real malice can exist side by side with skill or in an atmosphere where skill is respected.'[1]

That sounds like a formula for non-alienated work. Unfortunately for the craftsman, industrial society is no great respecter of traditional skills. Hand-loom weavers were amongst the first to be overtaken by technical innovations and made redundant. A few saddlers and loriners still exist, though their trades largely disappeared with the age of the horse. In more recent years most coopers have found that their skills are no longer required. Hanging over craftsmen there is always the threat that society will no longer have any use for their particular skill. Redundancy means more than a mere change of job. It is a blow at their status, at the basis of their self-respect, so well described in the above quotation.

Craft unions meet the threats of technological change with those same tactics which were once used simply to make their work scarce. As work changes they may, with varying degrees of success, still claim the exclusive right to such work. When a new machine is introduced, they may insist that only their members shall man it. This is called 'following the machine'. Within engineering the result has been that although a new set of skills is required, many of these jobs are still claimed by the AUEW. Shipwrights are a good example of men who have held onto work despite a

---

[1] *Machinery*, Sept. 23, 1915. Quoted by James Hinton in '*The First Shop Stewards Movement*' (Allen & Unwin, 1973) p 97.

change in material, in their case from wood to metal. Craftsmen may still claim work on occasion when it requires little skill of any sort. The term used to describe attempts to control workshop practice is 'ideological trade unionism'. It is much more prevalent in craft unions.

Two interrelated factors, which must be considered together, help to determine whether or not craft unions will prevail. They are the degree to which an industry becomes capital-intensive, and the sheer rate of technological change. Given rapid development of capital-intensive methods it is likely that craft unions will lose ground. Gas was our first capital-intensive, continuous-flow industry. Gas stokers could fairly claim to have skills as rare as those of many craftsmen, but they were not recruited into a craft union. A gas stoker could not possess the tools of his trade. He had less economic independence than, say, a carpenter, and his work was more alienated in this respect. But gas was also a completely new industry with a technology unlike any other. It had not evolved gradually so as to allow existing craftsmen to follow the machine. Many engineering sectors were capital-intensive and craft unions had managed to prevail through a slower rate of evolution.

The construction industry affords another important example. Nearly all houses are built in an extremely traditional manner. Raymond Postgate in his classic *The Builders' History*[1] notes that the tools and methods of a plasterer have hardly altered since they were used to line the pyramids of ancient Egypt. Bricklaying and joinery might not be quite so ancient but they have not been much affected by the industrial revolution. Craft unions dominate that section of the industry. Civil engineering by contrast employs the revolutionary method of ferro-concrete construction. Many, though not all, skilled men in this section belong to a General Union. When a new capital-intensive industry suddenly emerges it is not likely to be craft-

---

[1] Published by The National Federation of Building Trade Operatives, London 1923.

dominated. Such industries, as we shall see, tend to go to General Unions.

An important point to notice is whether or not a worker can easily find alternative employment at his own trade. Bricklayers and joiners may still possess all the tools of their trade and move fairly easily between a number of small firms. A toolmaker cannot reasonably expect to own the expensive machinery his trade now requires. At the same time, he can usually choose between a large number of tool-rooms in the same area. As craftsmen have to some extent controlled the design of jobs, they have left themselves with a wider choice of alternative employers. Given this fact, craft unions tend to have greater bargaining power, and it is relatively easy for them to make their work scarce as regards an individual employer.

Craft unions have a further advantage in that a small number of their members can often halt production. Only a few electricians may be involved in a strike which closes a whole factory. Union funds are sufficient to maintain the men on strike almost indefinitely. Craftsmen tend to hold key or vital positions within industry. This advantage is referred to as the 'strategic bargaining power' of craft unions.

Not surprisingly, craft unions have great faith in free collective bargaining and they concentrate their efforts in this direction. They now support the Labour Party and not the Liberal Party but there is a noticeable difference in emphasis from that of some other unions. Craft unions tend to have greater confidence in their industrial power and greater suspicion of government intervention.

General Unions

A General Union is the most open type of all: workers in any grade or craft from any industry are eligible for membership. The basic theory of General Unions has been called that of 'one big union'. This theory may become a practical proposition when all these different workers in reality have the unity of interests which it demands. After a false start in the 1830s, closely associated with Owenite Socialism, General Unions were formed again, in the 1890s, in another period of turmoil associated with a socialist revival. This time they held on, although with some difficulty in their early years. The 'New Unions', as they were called, carried the slogan 'Trade Unions for all'. In practice they were successful in recruiting all grades in new industries, such as gas and transport, but they were commonly associated with labourers and the semi-skilled, as indeed they are to this day. Casual labourers, or those who work in very small groups, have continued to present them with difficulties. Their great areas of strength are where there is a large number of workers with highly alienated work. For this reason at least one writer has seen their establishment as waiting upon the development of a proletariat, that is, an alienated social class as defined by our first chapter. If that is true it had not developed very far by the 1890s, but recent tendencies lend support to the argument.

Right up until the 1940s General Unions functioned largely as clearing houses; they tended to fill the gaps between other types of union. Since the 1940s structural changes in industry have favoured their original concept. One General Union, the 'Transport and General' is by far the largest in the country and is well established in mass-manufacturing industry.

G. D. H. Cole, the great labour historian, saw the logic of this development as long ago as 1942, when he pointed out that workers on the mass-manufacture of motor cars, say Fords, had much more in common with workers on the mass-manufacture of refrigerators than those at Rolls Royce. The Transport and General Workers' Union have succeeded in making large inroads into the motor-car industry, which rather frustrates the intention of the craft-dominated AUEW to become *the* union for all engineering workers. Economies of scale continue to create large plants using highly industrialised labour. A unity of interest is created amongst large numbers of workers doing a similar type of work in a variety of industries, and this is suited to the formula of General Unions. Where an industry is well defined, as in the case of coal or steel, then General Unions meet a hard frontier. That type of industry appears better suited to industrial unions. Industry, however, is tending to become less well defined. It is a moot point as to whether synthetic fibres belong to the textile industry or to petrochemicals. John Hughes, who did research for 'Donovan', has shown that what he calls 'the natural growth pattern' of British trade unions in the ten years to 1967 has favoured the more open type of union.

General Unions have a fairly distinguishable behaviour pattern based upon industrial logic. They do not commonly possess the strategic bargaining power of craft unions and they are much more vulnerable to economic recessions. Rather more emphasis is placed on their connection with the Labour Party. That is not to say that their historical origins in a period of socialist revival are unimportant. They were the first unions to include socialist objectives in their constitution. But they have moved from Marxist connections to being Labour 'moderates'. That shift is easier to understand if we take a look at industrial and economic circumstances.

It is rare for General Unions to be able to control workshop practice as craft unions do. Working in large-scale industry with highly alienated jobs, their members have little control to lose as compared with craftsmen. Even when they are promoted to fairly skilled work, it tends to be peculiar to their present employers. Craftsmen bring their skills with them and can soon take them to another employer. General Unions tend towards 'instrumental trade unionism': instead of aiming for workshop control they are more concerned with questions of wage rates.

Productivity bargaining essentially means accepting changes in working practices in exchange for higher pay. Since he who is at the bottom need fear no fall, General Unions are more prepared to consider this type of bargaining than craft unions. They are generally more amenable to new technologies, since these, by creating new skills, can break craft monopolies and thus enhance their members' prospects. Capital-intensive industry, all other things being equal, can afford to pay higher wages from its higher productivity per man. Dockers belong to the Transport and General and, with their strong resistance to containerisation, they make an important exception to the rule, though not the only one. Their union, however, has had great difficulties with this group of members for most of its history. Dockers have never fitted very well into the pattern of General Union behaviour, and many of them formed an important breakaway union (The Blue Union). As exceptions, then, they do seem to prove the rule.

Strategic bargaining power is only given to a minority of general workers. Strikes tend to involve large numbers and place a heavy strain on union funds as they drag on. This fact as much as any other accounted for the failure of General Unions in the 1830s as well as the subsequent decision of New Model Unions to go it alone. From their days as 'clearing houses' they have a large proportion of members with scarcely any bargaining power at all. Many workers in local government could be left out on strike almost indefinitely—park keepers and gardeners for example. A word of caution is necessary here because some workers who were thought not to possess any bargaining power have proved the opposite. Dustmen were thought to be in a weak position, until in London they left garbage piled high and everyone suddenly saw how vital they were to public health. Hospital workers have also only recently been moved to take industrial action, with some success from their point of view.

Nevertheless, it remains generally true that this type of union covers those groups of workers with little bargaining strength. General Unions have in membership most of the workers under Wages Councils, that is, those whose weak position is recognised by the Government and who therefore have a minimum wage fixed legally. Consequently, General Unions place more emphasis on political activity and are more prepared to see Government intervention.

In 1974 it was noticeable that the leaders of Britain's two largest General Unions were the staunchest supporters of the Labour Party's Social Contract. Craft unions gave it a cooler reception.

From their earliest years General Unions have been shown to be extremely vulnerable to economic recessions. Born in 1889, they all but disappeared in the slump of 1892. With every slump they have lost members as quickly as they gained them in a boom. Their members are the first to be laid off and the first to be taken on again. Although full employment policies are important to all unions, General Unions are more acutely aware of the need than most. Herein lies another reason for this type of union to look for Government regulation.

Outright socialists played a large part in New Unionism. New Unions, as already mentioned, were the first to adopt socialist objects. Within the TUC they were influential in persuading that body to adopt a resolution in 1899 which led to the formation in the following February of the Labour Representation Committee, which became the Labour Party in 1906. Always independent of the TUC, there is still no doubt that the Labour Party owes its formation to that resolution and subsequent strong backing from trade unions.

Originally, General Unions were closely associated with the revolutionary element in the LRC. But when times might be thought ripe for revolution, when there was a slump and great industrial discontent, these were the times when General Unions, as already explained, were at their weakest. They proved to be but a frail vessel for extreme socialist views. Their dependence upon reforms from Parliament has drawn them ever closer to those with gradualist opinions. They now stand somewhere about the centre of the Labour Party, in other words, for reform and not for revolution.

Bonds with the Labour Party are tight; for many years the Labour Party was housed by the Transport and General. Two General Secretaries of the Transport and

General have held cabinet office in Labour Governments. Will Thorne combined being General Secretary of the General and Municipal with being a Labour member of Parliament, as did other officials of that union. And so one could go on, but the point should have been made: a union with limited bargaining power, vulnerable to economic recessions, is inclined to seek remedies through reformist politics.

Industrial Unions

There are two ways of defining an industrial union. One is that it is a single union covering all workers in an industry. If that definition is adopted, then there are no industrial unions in this country. Another is that these are unions which seek to organise all workers in one industry. Under the latter definition we can place quite a number of British Unions in this category. Since it seems better to have a category that we can put something in rather than one which must remain empty, the latter definition will be used in this book.

The success of Industrial Unions depends mainly on whether there is, as a matter of fact, a unity of interest within each industry. A unity of interest comes from a wide variety of factors and nowhere is this more amply demonstrated than in the case of successful industrial unions. Members tend to have a great deal in common which goes beyond their occupation. Railwaymen and mineworkers have been referred to by sociologists as forming sub-cultures: in plain language, they are simply different from the rest of us. The National Union of Railwaymen and the National Union of Mineworkers are our best examples of successful industrial unions. Mineworkers come pretty close in fact to being the only union in that industry and their case will be taken first.

A typical mining village is dominated by the local pit. Nearly all the men work there as did their fathers and as will their sons. Many of these villages are fairly isolated and if they have a feeling of belonging, it is to a coal-mining region. The social centre of this village is also the union headquarters, extended to provide recreational facilities. Mining is the life-blood of the community. Union rules tend to be reinforced by social sanctions. In the past this might mean women of the village banging dustbin lids when any strike-breaker walked by. Mining is also an extremely dangerous occupation. If men do not co-operate closely and observe working rules, they may lose their lives. A high degree of conformity is a condition for survival. Outside management, a coal-face worker has the highest earnings but this is only one phase in a miner's career. Having worked their way up to this position, miners realise that as they get older such physically demanding work will be too much for them. They will have to come away from the coal face, perhaps to become surface workers. If they are lucky. Mining conditions are such that they are just as likely to be forced away from the coal face by injury or disease. The differential in earnings which coal-face workers enjoy is temporary, and how temporary none of them knows. There is a total contrast here with craftsmen in other industries who expect to keep their higher earnings for their entire career. This fact helps to explain the concern of miners for the lowest-paid in the industry, and the absence of craft unionism. No doubt there is an element of altruism here, though I would hesitate to suggest that miners are more altruistic than craftsmen. More credible as an explanation of this concern is their social cohesion, a 'togetherness', resulting from features of life in total in a mining village.

Uniformity nationally is created by the dominance of one technology and one employer. Unwilling though miners are to abandon their tight-knit communities, they can take their trade to other pits, as they have been forced to do by the closure of many pits in the 1960s. There are some regional differences: seams may be more difficult to work, the type of coal may be for export or home consumption. When productivity bonuses were proposed, areas with the easiest seams were keenest on the idea and voted in favour.

In the event, however, a majority were against the idea and that verdict was accepted. National solidarity has tended more and more in recent years to overcome regional differences. A high degree of regional autonomy is nevertheless still a feature of the NUM as compared with other unions.

Since the industry was nationalised there has, of course, been only one employer. National bargaining is the obvious answer to one national employer and there is one national agreement covering miners' wages in Britain. Advocates of industrial unions often neglect the importance of this factor in forging a unity of interest amongst employees.

When we look at railways we find that here too, there is one employer and one technology. The railways have also been nationalised and bargaining is on a national basis. Railway systems call for one technology so that a train can proceed easily to any part of the country on the same track through the same signals. During periods of change, two technologies may be used together, e.g. diesel and electric trains, but the ultimate aim is always for unification. Consequently there is one set of job requirements, giving one set of trades. Each trade finds itself working for one employer under similar conditions, which as a matter of common sense calls for one collective agreement.

Between trades, and this is where railways differ from mining, there is a possible division of interests. Footplate staff, originally drivers and firemen, form a quite distinct group. A fireman was an apprentice driver. Firemen have gone, but a train driver is still comparable to the craftsman in industry. There is still a form of apprenticeship and men over a certain age may not be trained for the job. Train drivers form an élite and the occupation is not merely one phase in a railwayman's career, as is the case with the coalface worker. Footplate staff have their own union, ASLEF. The NUR has never given up its ambition to take these trades into membership and there are some drivers in that union.

Even within the NUR there have been difficulties with signalmen, some of whom have formed a breakaway union. Having a highly responsible job and faced with increasingly complex systems, signalmen are not happy with their earnings differential. In spite of these reservations, the NUR is still a highly successful industrial union. Apart from footplate staff, it is *the* union in railways, although some maintenance workers, electricians for example, prefer a craft union.

The NUM and NUR make an interesting comparison because they show how a unity of interest can arise or fail to arise throughout an industry. A point to bear in mind with industrial unions is that one cannot 'put the cart before the horse'. Theory plays its part in creating an industrial union but it cannot create the sort of solidarity which arises from industrial facts.

Bargaining strength varies between industries. Coal is a vital source of national energy, and so miners have great bargaining power. Workers in the garment trade are in a relatively weak position: if they were to call a strike, we could all make do with the clothes we have. Much power and influence accrues to the great industrial unions we constantly hear about, the NUM and the NUR. Not so frequently mentioned is the National Union of Tailors and Garment Workers, which is also an industrial union. Their members have to have their wages propped up by a Wages Council, i.e. by law. The same is true of another industrial union, the National Union of Agricultural Workers.

It cannot be denied that union officials with only one industry to deal with have a great advantage. Other officials cannot hope to match their familiarity with technical and financial matters, at least not in every industry that they cover. Intimate knowledge of an industry does assist union officials to participate in policy making. Theoretically, industrial unions have been seen as a first step to more advanced industrial democracy.

Industrial unions are also thought to lead to more

responsible collective bargaining. Evidence to support this claim is usually taken from West Germany which has fewer industrial disputes than the UK. In Britain there is evidence pointing in both directions, for and against the proposition that industrial unions would give better industrial relations. A good deal depends, of course, on what you mean by 'better industrial relations'. But looking at coal mining we can see that a vast programme of rationalisation and modernisation was carried through with the co-operation of the NUM. A similar programme was carried out in Electricity Supply with no more difficulty, and yet here there is a multi-union situation led by a very powerful craft union, the EETU. Progress in shipbuilding has been retarded by demarcation disputes (who does what job), but most of them have been between two sections of the same union, the 'Boilermakers'.

If shipbuilding is to be quoted, then industrial unions offer little hope of solving disputes between trades. Difficulties with signalmen in the NUR and dockers in the Transport and General have been mentioned in other contexts. They are clear evidence that if there is not in fact a unity of interests, putting workers in the same union has little effect. Advocates of industrial unions may put too much emphasis on inter-union disputes, forgetting the disputes which occur when groups with different interests are in the same union.

As the last Royal Commission on Trade Unions and Employers' Associations ('Donovan'—published in 1968) pointed out, there are two multi-union situations. In the first, each of the main occupational groups is organised by a different union. There is therefore no argument about which union a group should belong to. In the second, more than one union claims to represent the same group of workers. This is likely to give rise to inter-union disputes.

In fact, disputes about which union a worker should belong to account for only 5% of industrial stoppages at the most. Nevertheless, the British union structure might still be made more rational. At present too much seems to be historically determined. Theoretically, industrial unionism has held the field as offering the best type of structure until quite recently and it seems appropriate to tabulate the major points for and against here, although some will only be fully apparent later in the book.

Arguments advanced in favour of industrial unions

1 Different unions would not attempt to recruit the same group of workers, thus coming into conflict with each other.

2 Unions would not compete with each other in militancy or obduracy in order to attract members.

3 Demarcation problems would be more easily solved.

4 One collective agreement would harmonise the claims of different sections.

5 Shop stewards in a plant would all be in the same union and would not have to meet unofficially.

6 Officials would only be concerned with one industry and therefore more familiar with its peculiarities.

7 Progress towards industrial democracy is easier with a responsible set of union representatives loyal to their industry.

Counter arguments

1 An industry can be very difficult to define. The coal industry and the railways are exceptional in having one technology, one product and one employer. Is engineering one industry? Or is there an aircraft industry, an automobile industry, an electrical appliance industry, and so on? Are synthetic fibres part of the chemical or textile industries?

2 Employers are not separated on an industrial basis, however it is defined. Firms like ICI and Unilever cover a range of industries.

3 An occupational analysis is more logical. Semi-skilled workers in mass-manufacturing across the industrial spectrum have a lot in common.

4 The structure of industry is constantly changing. Chemical firms now make synthetic fibres, houses are being made in factories. Unions which are more open are able to move into these new areas.

5 The Boilermakers' Society is an amalgamation of a number of unions and demarcation disputes persist.

6 One collective agreement does not necessarily harmonise the claims of different groups—witness the NUR's difficulties with signalmen.

7 One union does not necessarily prevent an unofficial shop stewards' movement. The Transport and General had such a movement in the London Docks.

8 The bargaining power of workers in some industries is negligible, for example in agriculture and the garment industry. General unions can develop a strong organisation and an efficient service from their other power bases.

9 General unions would never agree to their own dismemberment.

White-collar unions

This type of union is exclusively for non-manual workers. Occupational white-collar unions recruit members with particular jobs and professions regardless of industry; ASTMS, taking in scientists, technicians and supervisors, is a good example. An industrial basis is obvious with the National Union of Bank Employees and the National Union of Insurance Workers. Since they cover all grades in what are virtually white-collar industries, they might easily be classed as industrial unions. A third group restricts membership to certain occupations within one industry. There are several unions all catering for different grades in the Civil Service. A union may come into this category *de facto* by its choice of occupations: the Post Office Engineering Union is one example, and the National Union of Teachers is another, if you will allow education to be called an industry.

The National and Local Government Officers Association (NALGO), our largest white-collar union, is different again. It was formed originally from all white-collar grades in local government. When gas and electricity were nationalised, a number of municipal undertakings were taken over. NALGO members found themselves with new employers but kept their union cards. A similar thing happened with the formation of the National Health Service. NALGO therefore found itself with members in a number of industries. Outside local government, however, their range of grades is limited. Consequently, NALGO is partly occupational and partly industrial.

Finally we must remember that General and Industrial Unions are open to white-collar workers. When they are given complete sections to themselves, these sections are often classified as white-collar unions, although this is not strictly correct since they are not self-governing.

Since these people do not perform industrial work nor, at first sight, appear to be threatened by it, the reason for their trade unionism is not immediately apparent. In fact it is not only the man on the shop floor who is affected by aspects of alienation. David Lockwood in *The Blackcoated Worker*[1] attributes the rise of white-collar unions largely to bureaucratisation. An ugly word , it refers to the remoteness of an individual from the rule-making which still governs his or her working life. Terms and conditions are fixed for large numbers in common employment. In this respect a clerk in a large office is in exactly the same position as a worker on the production line, and has as much need for collective bargaining. In 1900 the National Union of Clerks had only 82 members, but then, as Lockwood points out,

---

[1] See pp. 141–9, *The Blackcoated Worker* (Allen & Unwin, 1958).

the typical clerk had a close relationship with his employer. White-collar unions now account for almost all growth in total union membership.

Office workers are affected by technical innovation. Computers can make large numbers of clerks redundant. Clerks have suffered less than they feared because of a general increase in white-collar work, although the clerical unions still used a fear of computers in order to recruit members.

In this century Governments have intervened more and more in industrial relations. During two World Wars victory depended upon increased production, which depended in turn upon well-regulated collective bargaining. The general arguments which Governments put forward may not be directed particularly to white-collar workers, but their logic spills over to apply to such employees. At least, the Government's policy of encouraging collective bargaining seems to create a favourable climate in which employers are prepared to grant recognition to white-collar unions.

White-collar unions have not typically forced recognition from employers by taking strike action. For a strike to be successful, workers must usually first be organised into a union, though this was not true of the London Dock Strike of 1889; white-collar unions tend to gain most members *after* recognition. The reluctance of these workers to join a union before it is recognised has a number of possible explanations. Staff are commonly given much greater security of employment than other workers, which possibly makes them reluctant to risk losing their job through industrial action to gain recognition. Another general characteristic is their interest in promotion. It is thought that joining a union which is not yet recognised could harm an employee's promotion prospects.

After recognition white-collar unions show more concern over careers. This may take the form of insisting that appointments are first advertised internally. In the field of education, union representatives are normally included on appointment panels. Annual increments to increase an employee's salary with his length of service are the norm with office and professional workers. These were introduced before unions gained a foothold, and were meant to encourage staff to stay with the same employer. White-collar unions have generally accepted them, although they cut across the old union principle of 'the rate for the job', that is, the same pay regardless of length of service.

Since white-collar unions do form such a mixed bag it seems that a clear behaviour pattern is not to be expected, at least not so far as a distinct type of trade unionism is concerned. Clerks in engineering are likely to be more militant and, perhaps, more instrumental in their approach than, say, members of a union catering for senior professionals.

Trade union federations

A number of unions in an industry may come to a working arrangement called a 'federation' or a 'confederation' with its own constitution and rules. These terms may cause some confusion. The Confederation of Health Service Employees, for example, is a single union, and not the only one in that industry. Each union within a federation or confederation—as we are now using these terms—remains self-governing, although it is obliged to pay attention to the group's policy. The function of these industrial groups varies enormously, from merely running a summer school to being the effective body for national negotiations. Obviously, when an industrial union emerges, the confederation no longer has any function. The confederation in building disappeared when most of the unions amalgamated to form UCATT.

The most famous is the Confederation of Shipbuilding and Engineering Unions (CSEU). This body conducts national negotiations with two employers' organisations, one for shipbuilding and the other for engineering generally. It is divided into a number of regions, though its local significance is usually minimal. There are about thirty affiliated unions, (the number is continually diminishing through amalgamations) including craft, general and white-collar. At the same time it cannot be said that the 'Confed' has solved many of the problems of multi-unionism. As we shall see later, its authority has been undermined by the spread of plant bargaining, and it has never taken control of the shop steward movement.

Changes in trade union structure

'Trade union structure' is a special term referring to the distribution of total trade union membership between different unions. Changes in the structure of industry are reflected by changes in trade union structure. As older industries decline, cotton for example, so does trade union membership in that sector. The growth of trade unionism in recent years, on the other hand, comes from the expansion of white-collar work. Table 1 overleaf indicates the present distribution.

There are problems in trade union structures which do not solve themselves. By definition, General Unions overlap with other types of union; Industrial Unions intrude into the territory of Craft and white-collar unions. Any rationalisation of union structure must be limited by this difference of opinion as to what is the ideal arrangement. When unions of the same type amalgamate, this reduces the actual number without disturbing the status quo. Unfortunately, although the number of British unions has been considerably reduced in recent years (see Table 2), mainly through amalgamations, the structure may be less rational than it was previously. Amalgamations have not always been between unions of the same type or, indeed, between unions which appear to have much in common at all. We need to consider a number of factors which cut across industrial logic.

The economics of running a union have their effect. There is possibly a minimum size of union capable of providing the services now commonly expected. Larger unions can afford computers, research departments, the best legal advice, and so on. Just one of these items, a computer for example, is quite beyond the resources of a union with only a few thousand members. On this count, our smaller unions are under some pressure to survive.

Table 1

*Unions in the TUC with over 150 000 members
(end of 1974)*

Union	Membership
Transport and General Workers Union (TGWU)	1 857 308
Amalgamated Union of Engineering Workers (AUEW)	1 437 839
General and Municipal Workers Union (GMWU)	883 810
National and Local Government Officers Association (NALGO)	541 918
National Union of Public Employees (NUPE)	507 826
Electrical, Electronic, Telecommunications and Plumbing Trade Union (EETU/PTU)	414 189
Association of Scientific, Technical and Managerial Staffs (ASTMS)	356 502
Union of Shop, Distributive and Allied Workers (USDAW)	352 610
National Union of Teachers (NUT)	264 349
Union of Construction, Allied Trades and Technicians (UCATT)	257 796
National Union of Mineworkers (NUM)	255 296
Civil and Public Services Association (CPSA)	215 144
Society of Graphical and Allied Trades (SOGAT)	193 804
Union of Post Office Workers	190 000
National Union of Railwaymen (NUR)	172 558
	8 659 649

Note: Total TUC membership is 10 363 724 in 111 unions. Total membership in all unions is 11 755 000 in 491 unions.

From TUC annual report and DEP Gazette

Table 2

*TUC membership and numbers of affiliated
Unions (5-year intervals)*

Year	No. of Unions	Total Membership
1869	40	250 000
1874	153	1 191 922
1879	92	541 892
1884	126	598 033
1889	171	885 055
1894	179	1 100 000
1899	181	1 200 000
1904	212	1 422 518
1909	219	1 705 000
1914		(no conference)
1919	266	5 283 676
1924	203	4 328 235
1929	202	3 673 144
1934	210	3 294 581
1939	217	4 669 186
1944	190	6 642 317
1949	187	7 937 091
1954	184	8 093 837
1959	186	8 176 252
1964	175	8 325 790
1969	155	8 875 381
1974	111	10 363 724

Source: TUC Annual Report 1975

A small union concentrated in one industry may find itself involved in long strikes which put a severe strain on its funds. The National Union of Vehicle Builders was a small craft union established in the motor vehicle industry and with few members elsewhere. They were competing for members with both the AUEW and the TGWU, giant unions with large memberships outside that industry and, therefore, much more able to stand the costs of strikes to which the industry is prone. Long before they decided to join the TGWU, the NUVB were looking for a suitable amalgamation. The AUEW, with its aim to become the industrial union for engineering, cannot have been pleased with their choice.

Prior to the Trade Union (Amalgamations, etc.) Act of 1964 it was difficult to get the necessary vote from members for an amalgamation. That act has made it possible to do so with a simple majority of those voting. There has been a noticeable increase in amalgamations as a result. The big unions are always keen to increase their size and influence. They took advantage of the new law to make overtures to smaller unions without waiting upon events. Amalgamations became something of a fashion and were, at times, affairs of the moment which were not always justified by long-term considerations.

UCATT was formed by a series of amalgamations with the serious intention of becoming the industrial union for the building industry. The TGWU already had some interest in that sector, however, which they increased through amalgamation. The Plumbing Trade Union had already decided to merge with the EETU to form the EETU/PTU. There are now fewer unions in the building industry, but its trade union structure is no more rational. The EETU/PTU has a substantial membership in engineering quite outside its interest in building, and UCATT itself has a fairly extensive empire throughout many industries. The principal component of UCATT was the old ASW, a 'new model' craft union with members throughout industry, whom it has retained. The same story is repeated with other amalgamations in other industries, so that there has not been a marked trend towards industrial unionism. The case of the NUVB already mentioned also illustrates the same point.

Some amalgamations have been much firmer than others. Two unions in printing subsequently decided upon a 'divorce'. The AUEW is still a rather loose amalgamation with several rule books. The 'Boilermakers' have not eradicated disputes between their different trades, although they are all craftsmen. All told, one cannot say that the 1964 Act has proved to be an unqualified success. Those who have gained most from it have been the General Unions.

Strictly speaking, there are two ways in which unions can come together. An amalgamation in the legal sense allows a rather loose connection that the two original unions may eventually break if they do not succeed in agreeing on one rule book for all members. A 'transfer of engagements' is really a take-over by one union of another union's members. Thus former members of the NUVB are now members of the TGWU. Generally, however, when we speak of amalgamations we are referring to a reduction in the number of unions by their coming together in any form.

FURTHER READING

Trade union histories mentioned at the end of the previous chapter deal with the origins of the different types of union. On the same subject, *Labouring Men* by E. J. Hobsbawm (Weidenfeld and Nicolson 1968) has some penetrating essays which ought to be read.

On problems of union structure the following are useful:

Trade Unions edited by W. E. J. McCarthy, Part 3 (Penguin, 1972)
Trade Union Structure and Government by John Hughes, Royal Commission Research Paper No. 5 (HMSO, 1967/8).

QUESTIONS FOR DISCUSSION

1 Are industrial unions the best answer to problems of trade union structure?
2 What advantages and disadvantages do you see in belonging to a small union, say one with less than 100 000 members?

3

How are Trade Unions governed?

There is such a diversity of rules and regulations that hardly anything one says about trade union government will be universally applicable. A discussion has to proceed on generalisations, and to lean heavily on words such as 'generally', 'usually' and 'normally'.

Introduction

Behind trade union rule books is a set of principles similar to those of the United States constitution. As unions have pursued their specific objectives, practice has departed from theory. A growing professionalism shifts more power to full-time officials. Instead of government by members, there is government with the consent of members. In some ways trade unions never were comparable with democratic states. They were designed as 'one-party democracies', that is democracies without a formal opposition. This theory may now be more open to question as unions have changed and found themselves in different circumstances. Branch life has decayed in a different economic and social climate. This is a serious matter, since the branch was the basic building block of the whole democratic structure. All of this, however, does not add up to the death of democracy in trade unions. Rules are steadily updated and there are other restrictions on officialdom.

General principles

Trade unions were designed to be highly democratic institutions. Their notion of democracy was government by the members. Every member belongs to a local branch. Branches submit motions to a national conference and, if passed, they become union policy. National conference is composed of delegates from nearly every branch, excluding the very smallest —those with, say, fewer than twelve members. Only conference can alter union rules, including union objectives. Rule 8 of the NUM puts it very simply: 'the Government of the Union shall be by Conference . . .'

Democracy may be shaped in many ways, but the model which has been most influential for British trade unions is the constitution of the United States. Modern unions originated in the middle of the nineteenth century, when the United States provided a practical expression of working-class ideals. In Britain the working classes were still excluded from political life. Two important ideas which they took from this source were that there should be a separation of powers and a written constitution.

In the American model, powers are divided into legislative, executive and judicial. British unions separate the legislative and executive functions more clearly than they do the judicial. National conferences which meet every one or two years are the equivalent of a legislative assembly with the power to change rules and formulate policy. Separate and less frequent conferences for the revision of rules do not alter the basic principle. Executive councils carry out policies—hence their title. This distinction is vital to an active democracy, so that government is by the people, or members in the case of trade unions. Full-time officials come under the executive council, which itself may be full or part-time or a mixture of both.

The judicial function is to decide whether rules have been broken. In unions, branches may impose fines and executive councils may expel members (the ultimate sanction). There is a right of appeal from branches to the executive council and from there to national conference. It is difficult to generalise further. Sometimes there is a separate appeals committee. Clearly, an appeals committee is closest to the American model because it offers protection both from officialdom and the occasional whims of the majority as expressed by national conference. There is, though, no trade union institution comparable to the Supreme Court. No trade union president has met his Watergate; at least, not within the union.

A written constitution is intended to fix with a high degree of certainty individual rights and democratic procedures. Union rule books often go into extraordinary detail. Individual rights are set out, including rights to stand for election, take part in branch meetings, receive certain benefits, and to appeal against disciplinary measures. An official's salary is to be found in his rule book alongside a precise list of his duties. One may even find the publication dates of the union journal. Scarcely anything can be contemplated to which some rule will not apply. The lack of an independent judiciary is mitigated by such precision. No member is free to fly in the face of rules. Other members have recourse to the ordinary courts of law, and union executives have been compelled in this way to observe their own constitution. In the famous ETU case of 1961, the whole nature of the executive council changed after it was found guilty of electoral malpractice. Officials and other activists do well to have a very thorough knowledge of their union rules.

Objectives and their implications

Trade unions are purposeful bodies and not just democratic exercises. They tend to be judged by their members according to their success in obtaining specific objectives.

In general unions have three 'primary objects': to improve members' wages and conditions through collective bargaining; to further their members' interests through political activity; and, finally, to provide welfare benefits. The last mentioned need not detain us very long. Originating when there was no welfare state, it has become less important in recent years. One significant benefit is free legal aid. Unions pursue compensation in the courts for members made ill or injured at work.

Collective bargaining has modified the principle of direct democracy and blurred the separation of powers. Conference cannot dictate the outcome of negotiations. It is not possible to predict exactly how the other side will react and much will depend on the skill of union negotiators. With national negotiations at least a degree of professionalism becomes an important factor. Conference can only indicate its wishes in broad terms. Furthermore, some unions deal with thousands of firms. In the intervals between conferences, there is such a mass of negotiation that conference could not possibly review it all in any detail. Most executives have the power to sign agreements and to decide when to take industrial action. National conferences therefore tend to go by results rather than to dictate the precise manner in which negotiations are to be conducted. As a consequence executives must be seen as formulating policies on industrial tactics. They tend in fact to govern with the consent of their members.

Some rule books do state that between conferences the executive is to be regarded as the government of the union. They have in mind all the eventualities that conference has not foreseen. This applies equally to the union's political activities. When governments choose to consult unions, they obviously go to high-ranking full-time officials. As such consultation has been very much extended in recent years it has enhanced the power and prestige of these officials. Most members perhaps learn of what is being said or done on their behalf through the public media. This is quite different from the union having a set of opinions and attitudes based upon the direct democracy of branch meetings. If a union were to resort to the old methods it would miss many opportunities to influence government policy. Unions do on occasion call special conferences or conduct postal ballots, but these are both expensive and time-consuming. Unions cannot afford them too often, and governments would grow weary of such slow responses. In practice executives are often forced to respond fairly quickly. Bearing in mind that unions have fairly specific objectives, executive councils may not see any necessity to consult their members. But in any case the situation is that a professional body of men use their judgement to represent the best interests of their members. In this way they govern their unions, albeit with the consent of their members.

One should not exaggerate this tendency towards government by consent. Whilst it is a noticeable feature, there is still much direct democracy within unions. This will become especially apparent with regard to shop stewards, but they are largely outside the constitutional government of unions. There is also a variety of district or area committees which may exercise more or less control over detailed negotiations. One should see this as a question about British trade unions rather than a statement of fact.

Comparison with national government

Unions are already different from national governments in that unions have such fixed and specific objectives. National government only has regard to the well-being of its citizens in more general terms, and its objectives may alter radically according to the party in office. Inseparable from that point is the fact that trade unions, almost by definition represent a unity of interests, whereas democratic government, also by definition, represents conflicting interests. Membership of a union is, in principle at least, voluntary. Short of emigration, when it is permitted, membership of the state is compulsory. Given that a union's objectives are plainly stated in its rule book, that it is designed to cater for a special-interest group, and that membership is voluntary, one can begin to see why British unions have always regarded themselves as one-party democracies. They have to date seen no need for a formal opposition. Although, there are trade unions in the United States with oppositions, and although the debate does not end there, one must recognize that argument by analogy with national government is apt to be misleading.

A crucial question is how divisive are political objectives and policies? Printed objectives fall into two categories. The first type, calling for allegiance to a particular political philosophy is, in the British context, of no great significance. The NUR, for example, has as one of its stated aims, 'To work for the supersession of the capitalist system by a Socialistic order of society'.[1] British railwaymen have not as a matter of history felt thus enjoined to seize every opportunity to disrupt the capitalist system of production. Such idealism is of historical interest in that it indicates that union's origins in a brief revolutionary phase of trade unionism. An AUEW rule refers to 'producer co-operatives and one then recollects that its predecessor, the ASE, was formed in 1851 when trade unions still had some faith in that institution. It would be absurd to expect that every member of the AUEW still believed in producer co-operatives. The EETU rule book seeks the democratic control of industry by its workers, and that union has recently declared its opposition to schemes of participation. In short, there are a number of union objectives which are either 'dead wood' or do not carry the obvious implications for union policy.

A second type simply allows political activity. Object 8 of the ASTMS is 'To promote legislation in Parliament for the benefit of members'. Only anarchists could object to that objective and nearly every union allows itself this type of activity. Unfortunately, such an objective can run into party politics when a particular policy is adopted. The allegiance of all members or even of a majority is then open to doubt, given that national officials take a good deal upon themselves when dealing with governments. Both the Irish and British TUCs were opposed to their countries joining the Common Market, and yet in both countries a subsequent plebiscite gave an overwhelming majority in favour of joining. One can only conclude that many trade union members did not agree with the opinion which had been voiced upon their behalf. Quite recently, the British TUC has been involved in the Social Contract with the Labour Government. Now there are many trade union members who do not sup-

---

[1] NUR Rules, Rule 1 (4a).

port the Labour Party. Neither Conservatives nor Communists agree with all of that Government's policies on wage restraint and cuts in public expenditure. In the face of this type of evidence there may be a case for formal oppositions within trade union government. •

Closed shops cut clean across the voluntary principle. Workers are compelled to join a union under the terms of their contract of employment. Closed shops are the order of the day in nationalised industries, whch means that some workers would have to give up their trade in order to avoid union membership. There is in these cases a high degree of compulsion, and it is not reasonable to suppose that all members enrolled under these circumstances are necessarily in agreement with a union's stated objectives.

All three conditions for a one-party democracy may be questioned in this way. Stated objectives cannot always be taken to mean what they say and are liable to the widest possible interpretation. It has been proved that unity of interest does not determine members' opinions on some political questions. In fact executives have appeared to be out of line with a very substantial proportion of their members. Finally, the voluntary principle becomes less credible with the extension of closed shops. There is a case to be made for formal oppositions within unions at least so far as their political activities are concerned.

Trade policies are a rather different matter. It is possible to see there a much greater unity of interest. There is a real choice between unions in most cases. The craft-minded worker is not usually compelled to join a general union even under a closed shop agreement. A permanent opposition would appear to be irreconcilable with the very nature of a trade union, which is to achieve concerted action on behalf of a group with a special set of interests. Employers or even other unions take the role of the opposition. The whole debate continues.

The decline of branches

Rule books make it clear that it is not only the right but the duty of members to attend their branch meetings. The importance of branches in changing rules and formulating policy has already been described. Originally all national elections were conducted through branches. The branch was the basic building-block of the whole democratic structure.

Time has not dealt kindly with this idea. As unions have grown much larger, they have recruited members who are less committed and less inclined to give up an evening to attend a union meeting. A consequence of government by consent is that a union's success is often measured by the sheer size of its membership.

Members who join for economic gain do not always find the business of branch meetings of any great interest to them. Local branches may have members working in a number of firms covered by different agreements. The branch is not really competent to pass opinions on any particular agreement. It tends therefore to concentrate on more general matters which only interest the committed trade unionist. Some branches are based on places of work, but it is not a practical proposition for them all to be organised in this way. Craft unions in particular often have only one or two members in a particular firm, and these must be allocated to a local branch.

Social and economic factors play their part. Branch meetings have to compete with television and all the other diversions our society affords us. Working populations tend to be more dispersed, and travel to a branch meeting place can be a real problem. If branches are based on places of work, then it is possible to overcome this difficulty by holding meetings in the lunch hour or immediately afterwards. Some employers allow branch meetings during normal working hours.

Plant bargaining has become more widespread and this can undermine branch authority. Shop stewards prefer to hold mass-meetings at work to decide various questions. Ordinary members can well feel that they are playing an active part in their union without ever attending a branch meeting. This type of bargaining usually cuts across union lines so that a decision cannot be made in the branch of any one union.

As attendances have fallen off—a figure of 4% is often quoted—branches tend to become less representative. It follows that national conference itself, since it is a matter of branch representatives debating branch motions, may be out of line with the views of a majority of union members. Executives certainly think so, as on occasion they have simply refused to obey the wishes of conference and referred the matter to a postal ballot of all members. The tendency is for executive councils and other officials to be elected themselves by these postal ballots. Democracy by post may be more representative but it is hardly in the spirit of the founding fathers. It does not afford the same opportunity for voters to hear all the arguments and to ask questions as at branch meetings.

Other democratic safeguards

Closed shops apart, the extent of support for an executive is demonstrated by the number of members that a union has. Workers can, as the saying goes, vote with their feet. They can leave a union, maybe to join another or maybe to drop out of membership altogether. This is a fact of life that no union executive can afford to ignore. Whatever decisions they make, they must consider the effects upon their membership figures.

Although a formal opposition does not appear on executive councils, there are frequently members with well-known and differing political views. Commentators can observe only too well when union elections swing to the right or the left, and such results are not lost on other office-holders. Policies do tend to be modified as a result. There is in NALGO an 'action group' who make clear their opposition to that union's traditional style. Voters know when a candidate is a member of that group. This is not quite the same as party politics but it comes close to being a formal opposition so far as elections are concerned.

Finally, it should be remembered that union constitutions

are gradually altered to meet modern circumstances. This process may be slow and a bit behind the times, but it goes on. The EETU, for example, gives formal recognition to the power of shop stewards by calling special industrial conferences of these representatives. Postal ballots have been allowed and this system of gathering opinion is now extensively used on major questions. The theory of trade union government as described should not be regarded as fixed for all time. Trade unions are living, growing things which can adapt to changed circumstances. Discussions continue as to the precise way in which they should be altered.

FURTHER READING

Union Rule Books—particularly your own if you are a member. They make fascinating reading now that you know what to look for.

The System of Industrial Relations in Great Britain, by Hugh Clegg (Blackwells, 2nd. Ed. 1972); see Ch. 3.
Organisational Issues in Industrial Society, edited by J. M. Shepherd (Prentice Hall, 1972)
Trade Unions edited by W. E. J. McCarthy (Penguin, 1972)

QUESTIONS FOR DISCUSSION

1 Does the branch have a future?
2 Is professional trade unionism desirable?

4

What is an Employers' Association?

Firms in an industry may belong to an employers' organisation. These organisations represent the interests of employers in a number of ways. Not all of them deal with organised labour but instead may concentrate upon trade matters. By contrast, the Engineering Employers' Federation is concerned exclusively with labour relations, and this is the function which is relevant to this book. Very simply, we are dealing with a countervailing power to that of trade unions.

It is sometimes suggested that an employers' association is a sort of 'union for the bosses', quite forgetting that individual firms are already combinations of shareholders and that some firms possess greater bargaining power than any trade union. As firms continue to grow in size by the merger movement, the need for employers' associations becomes less apparent. Indeed some firms, such as Fords, which began their operations upon a large scale, have never felt the need to belong to an association. The same is true of nationalised industries. So far as unions are concerned, British Railways, as a single state-owned enterprise, forms a more compact countervailing power than could any association of the old railway companies. More accurately we should see employers' organisations as one form, and not necessarily the most potent, in which organized capital may deal with organised labour.

If we have to find a parallel organisation on the other side of industry, it would be better to choose a confederation of trade unions. In both cases the degree of co-operation falls short of total amalgamation. Individual firms or unions will be compelled to opt out if they receive any direction not approved by those to whom they are accountable, shareholders or union members. They both, therefore, tend to rely upon a consensus of opinion rather than a majority vote. Their basis is industrial although they differ on occasion as to how the industry is defined. The Confederation of Shipbuilding and Engineering Unions, for example, has to deal with a number of employers' organisations.

Origins

There have been employers' organisations since the Middle Ages, when they took the form of Merchant Guilds and Livery Companies. These Guilds and Companies were mainly concerned with trade questions, though at times they had to deal with labour problems. In those days, however, society believed in a 'just price' and a 'just wage'. The influence of any body that interfered with the 'natural laws of supply and demand' was bound to decline as society came to believe in the virtues of unrestricted competition. As a result their nineteenth-century counterparts claimed that they were forced into existence by the restrictive practices of trade unions. No-one has yet written a history of employers' organisations, but there is evidence that it was not always labour that took the initiative. At times and in places, it is true, one can see employers as reacting to union pressure. The best-known example is in the engineering industry, where employers have repeatedly countered union challenges. But in both the coal and iron industries, local associations of employers were regulating wages before there were stable trade unions. Furthermore, we must remember that unions arose in answer to the power of industrial capital organised into large joint-stock companies. One cannot, therefore, see employers' organisations as a necessary evil brought about by the activities of unions. It is better to see them both as components in a system which has arisen to deal with the industrial relations problems of modern society.

Structure

When trade unions were all on a local basis, so were employers' associations. You may remember that a characteristic of New Model Unionism was that it organised upon a national basis. Within one year of the founding of the Amalgamated Society of Engineers in 1851, employers in the industry from London and Lancashire (later to be joined by firms from Yorkshire) had formed the Central Association of Employers of Operative Engineers. This was the first occasion on which engineering employers had come together on anything other than a purely local basis. That association faded away but it was eventually succeeded by the Engineering Employers' Federation. A general upsurge at the time of New Unionism led employers in other industries to form national federations, notably the Shipping Federation, formed in 1890.

Present day structure reflects these historical origins. Firms affiliate to a local association which in turn belongs to a national federation. One must be careful about the terms, however, as some federations are local and some associations are national. Employers have lagged behind unions in this respect, because most organised workers are simply members of a national organisation with one rule book and one executive. On the employers' side many local associations are not affiliated as yet to a national group, and when they are they preserve a high degree of autonomy. This makes things very difficult for a multi-plant company which must join a number of local associations, perhaps with different policies. A much-needed reform is to allow these multi-plant companies to affiliate direct to the national federation. There are also examples of local associations which now have only one firm left in membership.

The autonomy of localities varies considerably. In electrical contracting, wages and conditions are effectively controlled by a Joint Industry Board, although some extra

payments are allowed on site under exceptional circumstances. Employers belong to 'branches' of their national
Electrical Contractors' Association, which does run parallel
to union organisation. At the other extreme, local port employers' associations negotiate their own agreements independently of the National Association of Port Employers.
Within the same organisation there may be variation, so
that, for example, the Liverpool Region of the National
Federation of Building Trade Employers has more autonomy
than other regions.

Nationally, federations cater for separate industries. The
problem sometimes is to define the industry. The EEF is
frequently criticised for trying to cover too great a diversity
of products. The whole of the motor industry is only supposed to form a part of the engineering industry. With
nearly 5000 firms in membership, the federation is thought
by some people to be far too cumbersome. There are committees to cover well-defined areas such as non-ferrous metals
but the industry is a difficult one to rationalise. Product
divisions can be found in some other federations, but a
regional or local structure is still the most prevalent.

It is commonly asserted that employers' organisations have
a more rational structure than do trade unions. That may be
true, but it is not a cause for complacency. There is much on
the employers' side that is out-of-date and far too complex.

Extent of employer organisations

The last Royal Commission into these matters, published in
1968, found some 1350 employers' associations listed by the
Department of Employment. In 1936 there were 1820 dealing with employment questions, whilst the corresponding
figure for 1959 was 1600. For the most part these consist of
local associations affiliated to national bodies. The Confederation of British Industry has more than a hundred
national federations in membership. Bearing in mind the
considerable variation in local autonomy it is not possible to
make a straight comparison with trade unions, but we must

reckon there to be many more employers' organisations than there are trade unions.

As to the number of workers covered there are only loose estimates. It is clear, however, that employers' organisations cover a greater proportion of the workforce than do trade unions. So far as firms are concerned, the majority are in membership. Large firms may not feel the need to join these organisations, and indeed may regard them as more of a hindrance than a help. Very small firms may not join for a number of reasons. A fairly common reason is that with their small labour force they can maintain a highly informal and flexible relationship with their employees. In the past employers' organisations have put pressure on firms to affiliate, but this is no longer the case. There is a certain social prestige attached to membership which is thought to be sufficient inducement.

Objectives

In the nineteenth century employers sometimes combined simply to destroy trade unions. That attitude was never universal, though it was certainly that of engineering employers in the great lock-out of 1852. Unions are now too well-established for this to be a feasible proposition. Owing to their political as well as economic influence, most governments, particularly in times of crisis, are anxious to have their co-operation. Government policy has done a lot to modify the approach of employers to trade unions. The present situation is that employers take concerted action in order to match the power of organised labour. To be more precise, they seek to influence the labour market to the advantage of their members. Against the upward pressure of trade unions on labour costs these organisations are concerned to maintain 'reasonable' profits for their member-firms. Related to this overall objective are four subsidiary aims: to regulate wage bargains; to provide for the peaceful settlement of disputes; to defend managerial prerogatives; and to set standards in labour relations. Each of these aims needs further discussion.

Negotiations lead to agreements applicable to all affiliated firms. Usually the rates of pay are minimal subject to improvement at local or plant level. The spread of productivity bargaining forced most organisations to adopt this formula. The gap between national rates and the average amount actually paid by firms has tended to increase appreciably in recent years. In engineering, this has led many critics to dismiss the national agreement as a pointless fiction. Other parts of the wage bargain, however, are more strictly adhered to, such as hours of work, holidays and premium payments for shift work or overtime. The agreement in the electrical contracting industry does fix standard rates of pay which may only be varied under certain specific circumstances.

The value of this type of agreement to employers is not simply to hold down wages. Affiliated firms are prevented from drastically undercutting the wage costs of their competitors. Unions help to maintain discipline in this respect, since they may refer to the association any firm that is not providing the required wages and conditions. When a union only has a few members inside a firm it would rather do this than attempt a confrontation. Trade unions, therefore, have some interest in maintaining employers' organisations.

The peaceful settlement of disputes is complementary to employers' other aims. Conciliation services within industry have a much longer history than is sometimes recognized. J. H. Clapham in *An Economic History of Modern Britain* refers to a Committee of Conciliation in the Potteries as long ago as the 1830s.[1] More famous is the Hosiery and Glove Trade Board of Arbitration and Conciliation set up between the employers' organisation and the trade union in 1860. During the First World War, the Government encouraged many other organisations to set up similar machinery.

The basic principle is that a dispute within a plant or firm may be referred to higher authority before industrial

---

[1] p. 173, Book 3, *An Economic History of Modern Britain* (Cambridge, 1963).

action is taken by either side. Typically, the first stage outside the firm is a local conference of employers and full-time officials. Representatives from member-firms may conduct the employers' side of the case or leave it to paid officials of their organisation. It really depends on how large and well-organised the employers' organisation is in that particular locality. If agreement cannot be reached then the matter may be referred to national level. Cases are sometimes referred back to a lower level for settlement. Obviously when this occurs too often the whole apparatus tends to lose credibility. Trade unions then feel that the conciliation procedure is simply a time-wasting exercise. A critical factor here is the amount of time that it takes to go through procedure. If it takes too long, workers on the shop floor may lose patience, especially when they find that after waiting for procedure to be exhausted their case is simply referred back for settlement.

'Managerial prerogatives'

This third aim means in plainer language, 'the right to manage'. Unions have in general sought to encroach upon managerial prerogatives and bring more decision-making under joint control. The subject is one that we shall return to when dealing with 'participation'.

Employers and their organisations vary considerably in their willingness to share power with the unions. Some have taken the initiative in schemes for greater participation, whilst others view the whole topic with a kind of horror. Different products give rise to different technologies and these in turn lead to different types of managerial organisation. At the same time there are different types of union to be considered, and we have already discussed their varying attitudes to workshop control. Federations and associations of employers are bound to reflect these differences in their experience. For example, engineering employers tend to have an impersonal type of supervision which is confronted by a craft-minded union keen to maintain traditional working rules. Not surprisingly, a struggle over the right to

manage has been a constant theme in the history of the
Engineering Employers' Federation.

General improvements in labour relations

In recent years some employers' organisations have established a labour relations leadership. Instead of simply reacting to events, they have sought to anticipate problems by
conducting research and employing more specialist staff.
One suspects that they may be trying to recover some of the
initiative they have lost through plant bargaining and increasing government intervention.

Unilateral action

However enlightened employers may be and however skilful
at negotiating with unions, the realities of power cannot be
ignored. Both parties at the negotiating table have in mind
the strength of the opposition. Employers may decide to risk
a strike rather than make further concessions. A trial of
strength ensues in which employers appear in a passive
role. Passive resistance is not the only tactic open to them.
They too have 'weapons' at their disposal, although they
are less obvious than those of unions.

A 'lock-out' means that firms refuse to allow their employees back to work until they have accepted certain conditions. If firms are united in this action it will clearly be
much more effective. We have noticed in passing the engineering lock-out of 1852. The great London lock-out in
the building trade in 1859 reduced the men and their
families to near-starvation. Engineering employers have
initiated an all-out power struggle on two other occasions,
in 1897 and 1922. They considered another general lock-out
in 1957, but the country was in the midst of the Suez Crisis,
and the Government intervened to prevent a major disruption of industry. Theoretically, this weapon is still available to employers' organisations, but it does not put them in
a good light so far as the Government or general public are
concerned. Individual firms still apply this sanction upon

occasion, although usually on a small scale, directing it at a particular group of their employees.

Some associations still offer a kind of strike insurance; the EEF is one of them. Provided that a firm follows the advice of the Federation, they are paid compensation during a stoppage based on the number of adult male workers involved. This insurance is something of a relic of the past. Today it is the moral support of fellow employers which is regarded as being much more important. One is left wondering, however, what exactly is involved in 'moral support'.

Historically, two other sanctions have occurred, though their use today is generally denied. One is the 'Black List', which is a list of militant trade unionists that employers in the organisation will not employ. The other is a 'No Poaching' agreement, whereby firms agree amongst themselves not to compete for certain specified types of labour. These are not published so that it is difficult to ascertain the extent to which they still exist.

FURTHER READING

The Power to Manage, by Eric Wigham (Macmillan, 1973), deals with the history of the EEF.
Employers' Associations by V. G. Munns and W. E. J. McCarthy, Royal Commission Research Paper No. 7 (HMSO. 1967/8)
Employers' Organisations and Industrial Relations, CIR Study 1 (HMSO, 1975).
Selected Written Evidence to Donovan from the CBI (HMSO, 1968).

QUESTIONS FOR DISCUSSION

1 Are employers' organisations likely to hold back progressive companies?
2 Do employers' organisations perform any beneficial function so far as trade unions are concerned?

5

The TUC and the CBI

Trade Union Congress (TUC) is the co-ordinating body for trade union opinion and the Confederation of British Industry (CBI) serves the same purpose for employers' organisations. When a government wishes to consult both sides of industry, these are the bodies to which it turns. As governments have intervened more and more in industrial relations the TUC and the CBI have attained greater prominence, and must now be familiar names to most members of the general public. Unfortunately, the precise nature of their authority is less clearly understood. Neither organisation is at the top of a chain of command in the same way as, shall we say, a board of directors. Both organisations strive to represent a broad consensus of opinion. This is why the phrase 'co-ordinating body' is appropriate.

Trades Union Congress

When the TUC was formed in the late 1860s, trade unions were already established amongst skilled workers, but they were involved in a struggle to obtain more political influence. Their objectives at this time were fairly narrow. Rather than seeking democracy in the same way as the Chartists, they were after specific legal reforms which were necessary to trade unionism. The Second Reform Act of 1867 had, in any case, given the vote to most craftsmen. The existing Master and Servant Law treated a worker who broke his contract of employment as a criminal. The very existence of trade unions was threatened by the Hornby v. Close judgement in 1867, which showed that they had no legal protection if their funds were misappropriated. Greater political influence was sought in order to persuade Parliament to pass legal reforms. The TUC's nature was evidenced by the title of Parliamentary Committee which they gave to their executive. This was changed to that of General Council in 1921. In today's jargon we would describe such an organisation as a political pressure group, and this is a role which the TUC continues to have.

The TUC, as mentioned in connection with General Unions, was prominent in the formation of the Labour Party at the beginning of this century. The TUC still has a special understanding with that party, and there is a liason committee between the two. But the TUC itself is not affiliated to the Labour Party. Individual unions choose which party, if any, to support. In fact there are many more unions affiliated to the TUC than to the Labour Party. None of this can disguise the fact that the TUC is a political pressure group. What does follow is that the TUC cannot be said to have a single political ideology. The situation is different in most other European countries, where there are a number of 'TUCs' according to their political or religious ideology.

Over the years political objectives have broadened. Workers have homes and families, and the TUC is keenly interested in social questions such as health and education. An interest in economic questions is fairly obvious. A consensus of opinion is not impossible on any of these specific questions when they have a bearing on workers' interests. However, the more remote a question is from the immediate interests of British workers, the less likely there is to be a TUC line. Certainly the TUC does not follow the Labour Party line automatically, despite the sympathy which it undoubtedly has with that party's policies. The TUC maintains its independent right to deal with governments of any complexion in furthering workers' interests.

In matters which do not concern the movement as a whole, individual unions are very much masters in their own house. They conduct negotiations with employers and sign their own agreements. Unions must report serious disputes to the TUC, which will then act in a conciliatory role. In 1926 the General Council called a special conference of trade union executives who committed their members to a General Strike. The TUC itself had no such powers. As a matter of fact neither did some of the union executives at the conference under their individual constitutions. The TUC proved to be a woefully inadequate agency for handling such a situation. When the General Council called the strike off, the miners carried on, as they had every right to do under their constitution. Not surprisingly the TUC is extremely reluctant to become involved in industrial disputes, except as a conciliator. It would be foolish to repeat the act of organising industrial action in support of a particular member-union, when they lack the power to compel that union to accept any terms of settlement.

Despite this lack of authority over member-unions, one must not underestimate the TUC's importance. There is the coincidence that leaders of the more powerful unions are all members of the General Council. When the Council is of one mind, these leaders possess considerable power to bring about the desired result through their individual unions. Secondly, as the body to which the government automatically turns for advice on union matters, the TUC has places on a number of important agencies and committees. Slow though the TUC may be to move into confrontation, when it does so it is in the confident knowledge that adequate consultations have ensured the support of one of the most potentially powerful trade union movements in the world. Consent must first be obtained from a diversity of unions but, given that consent, recent history has shown that the government can scarcely stand in its way.

The Conservatives' Industrial Relations Act, 1971, had this effect of closing the ranks. Not all unions were prepared to follow TUC policy, but they were suspended and then expelled on a scale never known before, which showed the determination of the movement as a whole. A famous cartoonist used to portray the TUC as an old cart-horse. Perhaps we should remember that although a cart-horse appears to be a rather docile animal, it is also an extremely powerful one. Not suited to racing or jumping, it can still pull quite a heavy load. Just how much pull the TUC has we can see by looking into its organisation and activities in more detail.

Annual Congress

Since 1868 affiliated unions have held an annual congress. It meets on the first Monday in September and remains in session for four days. The Chairman of the General Council presides. Congress has three functions: to consider the work of the Council over the previous year; to debate and vote on motions submitted by unions and the General Council; and to elect the next General Council. Well before Congress, delegates will have had a detailed report of the work of the Council. Each paragraph of the report is taken with any relevant motions.

Voting is usually by a show of hands, although a 'card vote' is sometimes called for. Cards are issued on the basis of one vote for every thousand members or fraction thereof. The point of this procedure is that some unions represent many more members than others and therefore should cast more votes. If this procedure were abandoned, unions would simply use their constitutional right to send one delegate for every five thousand members. This would present considerable practical problems so far as accomodation is concerned.

Although the General Council is not bound to follow the policies dictated in resolutions of Congress, they have to report back the following year on what action if any they have taken. If Congress is not satisfied a 'reference back' will be carried, and this is something which the General Council obviously wishes to avoid.

Congress takes place in a glare of publicity with reporters from newspapers, radio and television. Consequently it does have a direct effect upon public opinion. People tend to calculate the mood of the movement from what is said in debates and the way that voting goes. Anyone with a direct interest in industry will follow the proceedings carefully, since they are an indication of the line which unions will be following in the coming year. This is in marked contrast to the employers' side, which has no similar convention.

General Council

The composition of the General Council changes to take account of changes in industry and commerce. The year 1974 will provide an example of the fundamental principles involved. There were 38 seats on the General Council which were allocated to 18 trade groups plus one special group for women workers. Any union in a group may put forward nominations for that group, but the vote is taken from the whole of Congress. In this way the elected member is recognised as having particular interests but is not allowed to forget that he or she is responsible to the whole of Congress. Students of politics will recognise the American influence here with its system of 'checks and balances'. Not every group has the same number of seats. In 1974, the number varied from one to four according to the total of trade union members represented.

Minorities do not always succeed in getting a place on the Council. Two general secretaries of the National Union of Mineworkers were kept off because they were members of the Communist Party. The big unions, if they act together, may dominate elections because they have the majority of votes. For many years it was the right wing of the Labour Party which ruled the biggest unions and therefore the General Council. There was an exception, which arose because the ETU was the only union in its group; their Communist General Secretary was the only nomination and therefore had to be elected. Recent years have not seen the same concerted action from major unions, and the Council represents a much wider spectrum of opinion. All the same, the logic of the situation is that where a seat is contested by representatives from smaller unions, they must canvass the support of one or other of the 'big boys'.

Having been elected, the Council acts as the executive body of Congress under rules and standing orders. In the coming twelve months they will try to bring various resolutions into effect and deal with situations as they arise. If a particularly important crisis arises, they may call a special congress.

Committees

Each member of the General Council serves on a number of committees, such as 'Finance and General Purposes', 'Economic' or 'Education'. In addition there are a number of advisory bodies, including 'Women's Advisory Committee' and the 'Non-manual Workers Advisory Committee' on which representatives elected at special conferences contribute their knowledge and experience. These committees are given research and secretarial assistance by the appropriate department at Congress House.

Relations with Government

The Government includes trade unionists on their commissions and committees. The National Economic Development Council (NEDC) is a consultative body with representatives from Government, nationalised industries, the CBI and the TUC. Their opinions are sought on a wide range of economic and industrial problems. There are three bodies with equal TUC and employer representation which, although financed by the Government, are otherwise independent. The Manpower Services Commission is responsible for industrial training and employment services. The Health and Safety Commission was set up to implement the Health and Safety at Work Act. The Advisory, Conciliation and Arbitration Service does what its name suggests in the field of industrial relations.

Through these institutions the General Council exerts a direct and continuous influence upon national policies. In addition, General Council committees usually have no difficulty in contacting Ministers upon matters of importance to the movement. Taken altogether this influence with Government must form a considerable inducement to unions to join the TUC. This holds true for certain white-collar unions, which have no wish to be associated with the Labour Party but certainly wish to have the ear of Government.

Full-time Staff

A General Secretary is elected by Congress. He is not subject to annual re-election but remains in office for so long as his work is satisfactory to Congress and the General Council. By virtue of his office he is a member of both those bodies. The General Council appoint an Assistant General Secretary to assist him in his duties. Day-to-day administration is the responsibility of the General Secretary, and he appoints the remainder of the staff, who at present number about 120 at Congress House, with a further 25, approximately, throughout the country.

At Congress House, the TUC's headquarters, there are five major departments: Education, Organisation and Industrial Relations, International, Economic, and Social Insurance and Industrial Welfare. Each department serves one or a number of the above-mentioned committees. Five other departments deal with general administration and provide services for the General Council and staff: Press and Publications, Finance, Supplies and Services, Filing and Records, and the Library.

The Education Department is associated with a committee of the same name. They are mainly concerned with trade union education, though they also watch over developments in the employment and training of young persons. A considerable programme of trade union education is carried out through a variety of media, including the TUC's own college at Congress House, postal tuition, week-end and summer schools, and day-release courses in Technical Colleges and other institutions. Training for shop stewards and safety representatives are good examples of the type of work undertaken.

The Organisation and Industrial Relations Department

serves a number of committees which illustrate the range
of its functions: Organisation, Employment Developments
Policy, Trades Councils, Local Government, Non-Manual
Workers, Wages Councils, Health Services, Women's
Advisory, and, finally, the Disputes Committee, about
which more will be said in connection with inter-union
disputes. In general this department deals with problems of
trade union organisation at national level and it also makes
arrangements for annual Congress.

Relations with overseas counterparts of the TUC, world
organisations of unions, and the International Labour
Organisation are maintained by the International Department with its two associated Committees, the International
and the Commonwealth Advisory. This aspect of TUC
work is given fuller attention in Chapter 6.

The Economic Department also serves a wide range of
committees dealing with economic problems at national
and industrial level. These include the TUC side of the
National Economic Development Council. Each year the
TUC produces an Economic Review, which surveys current
trends and makes policy recommendations.

'Social Insurance and Industrial Welfare' is the title
of a department and a committee. Another committee is
the Advisory Committee of the TUC Centenary Institute of
Occupational Health. This department not only deals with
those matters mentioned in its title, but also takes environ-
mental issues under its wing.

Inter-Union Disputes

The most common cause of disputes between unions is
disagreement over which union a group of workers should
belong to. To solve these membership problems the TUC
has a panel of General Council members and other experienced officials from which a Disputes Committee will be
drawn, none of whom are directly interested parties. This
committee operates under the Bridlington Principles,
named after the venue of the 1939 Congress at which they
were adopted. These rules require affiliated unions to check

whether an applicant is or has recently been a member of another union. They may not accept into membership anyone who is under discipline, engaged in a trade dispute or is in arrears with contributions to his former union. Furthermore, no union should start organising at any establishment where another union 'has the majority of workers employed and negotiates wages and conditions, unless by arrangement with that union' (Principle 5). Awards of Disputes Committees are published in the TUC's annual report.

At a Special Congress held in Croydon in 1969, the TUC was given greater powers in respect of any inter-union dispute, whether official or unofficial. No affiliated union should authorise a stoppage of work over an inter-union dispute until the matter has been considered by the TUC. Where an unofficial stoppage is in progress, the union concerned must use its best efforts to obtain a resumption of work. Under the Croydon procedure, the TUC can take action on any inter-union dispute including those to do with demarcation or conditions of employment.

Although this machinery does not provide a perfect answer to all inter-union problems, there is no doubt that it does serve to prevent unnecessary stoppages of work and keeps some semblance of order in the conflicting claims of the various unions which are affiliated to the TUC.

Disputes between unions and employers

Decisions taken at the Croydon Special Congress covered disputes with employers. Unions must notify the TUC when they become involved in a serious industrial dispute, that is, one that is likely to affect a substantial number of workers or which will have serious consequences if it lasts a long time. The General Council, however, will not usually intervene whilst there is any prospect of the parties directly concerned being able to solve it.

The TUC does have the power to investigate a dispute which has not been reported. If the TUC's advice is ignored in any case, the matter will be reported to the next Congress.

The TUC was very active in trying to help solve the sea-men's dispute with their employers in 1976 since it threatened to break the Social Contract.

None of this should be construed as contradicting the earlier statement that unions are masters in their own house so far as negotiations are concerned. When agreement is finally reached, it will be signed by the employers and unions concerned, but not by the TUC. If unions decide to ignore TUC advice, the worst that can happen to them is that they will be expelled from the TUC.

TUC Industrial Committees

These are a fairly recent innovation, dating only from the nationalisation of the steel industry in 1967. Since then a number of committees have been set up to cover other industries. All affiliated unions within an industry provide representatives for a committee to co-ordinate policy on recruitment, holidays, sick pay and so on. Although these committees take responsibility for their own decisions, the TUC staff service them and so are much more involved than formerly in the actual business of bargaining with employers. Apart from being connected with the TUC, Industrial Committees are very similar to Confederations. The involvement of TUC staff may, however, prove to be highly significant in the long run if it is a step towards a more integrated industrial policy on the part of British trade unions.

Confederation of British Industry

The CBI was founded by Royal Charter in 1965. Three national employers' organisations were thus amalgamated and representatives from the nationalised industries were added. Two of the employers' organisations were mainly concerned with commercial matters: the National Associa-tion of British Manufacturers (previously the 'National Union of Manufacturers') and the Federation of British Industries. The third, the British Employers' Confederation, was mainly concerned with labour matters and was seen as the employers' counterpart of the TUC. Today, the CBI is very much involved in general trade matters in both national and international terms, but it is their function in the field of industrial relations with which we are mainly concerned. Their forerunner in this respect was the British Employers' Confederation, and this is the body which has bequeathed a certain tradition to the CBI which is only changing slowly. Henceforth in this section to avoid difficulties over its change of name it will be referred to simply as the Confederation.

Origins

It is worth while noting that all three employers' organisations were formed in response to government intervention. This is a theme that we shall see repeated throughout the history which led up to the formation of the CBI, and which is still highly relevant in some respects. The National Union of Manufacturers was founded in 1915 and the Federation of British Industry in 1917, under the conditions of war-time regulation of industry. The Confederation was originally the employers' side of the National Industrial Conference summoned by the Government in 1919.

As the Government withdrew from intervention after the war, the Confederation faded from view. Following the General Strike in 1926, there was at least one episode when they might have attained a prominent position in the British system of industrial relations. The Confederation's rejection of the famous Mond-Turner proposals of 1928[1] effectively denied Britain anything like a centralised system of collective bargaining such as they have in Sweden. At the 1927 Trades Union Congress, the president regretted the failure of national organisations to establish effective machinery for consultation and negotiation.

At first employers' organisations ignored the hint, but Sir Alfred Mond (later Lord Melchett), who was chairman

---

[1] TUC Annual Reports, 1928, pp. 209-30; and 1929, pp. 188-204.

of the newly formed ICI, brought a group of leading industrialists to meet Ben Turner, then Chairman of the General Council of the TUC. From these talks emerged a number of proposals for the improvement of industrial relations, including the setting up of a National Industrial Council consisting of representatives from the TUC, the Confederation, and the Federation of British Industries. Although the Federation of British Industries along with some of the larger firms and those employers' associations influenced by Lord Melchett were in favour of these ideas, the Confederation most certainly was not. The Engineering Employers' Federation had a powerful voice in the affairs of the Confederation, and this Federation was involved in its usual duel with engineering unions over managerial prerogatives. The Confederation saw the TUC as being politically motivated and basically opposed to private enterprise. They would only accept consultation with the TUC in the interests of employers' unity, not in the interests of the Mond-Turner proposals.

When all three organisations finally met in 1929, the TUC was informed that the two employers' organisations had such different responsibilities that they could not enter into a single National Industrial Council. The TUC was invited to consult with either body, with the other then deciding quite independently whether to accept any ensuing recommendations. Nothing was to trespass on the autonomy of the individual organisations. This arrangement was accepted but proved quite ineffectual and soon fell into disuse. Thus the opportunity to participate with the TUC in formulating national industrial policies was firmly rejected by the Confederation. Ironically, the result had to be to make the TUC more 'political' since it was then forced to approach governments on questions of national minimum standards for conditions of work.

Only very gradually did the Confederation emerge into public view or have much to do directly with the TUC. During the Second World War, the Confederation was represented on a wide range of consultative bodies which were set up to improve industry's war effort. They were over-shadowed, however, by the prominent part played by labour leaders, such as Ernest Bevin, in the war-time coalition. Their reticence to appear on the public stage did not really begin to break down until the mid-fifties, when their concern with inflation caused them to issue a pamphlet on 'Britain's Industrial Future'.

One may note in passing that inflation, along with state intervention, has been one of the twin causes most likely to prompt the Confederation or its successor to public pronouncement. In 1956 the Confederation was involved in discussions which the Government held with a number of organisations and which subsequently led to the 'price freeze' of that year. In 1961 the Confederation went so far as to invite a representative of the TUC to a conference on industrial relations. Broadly speaking, the conference came down in favour of plant bargaining. In line with that decision the Confederation recommended the following year that shop stewards should be given time off with pay to attend training courses. By 1964 the Confederation and the TUC were involved in joint investigations into the causes of unconstitutional strikes.

This trend was given a significant push by the Government when in 1962 they established the National Economic Development Council, which covered commercial and industrial matters. The TUC automatically provided trade union representatives for this body but there were still three separate employers' organisations which could claim an interest. The Government in fact solved the problem for a time by simply inviting prominent industrialists to sit on the Council. Given the authority and influence of the NEDC, however, this was not a satisfactory solution since it ignored the employers' own organisations. Eventually the separate organisations came together in 1965 to form the CBI.

Membership

The CBI admits to membership employers' associations, trade associations, individual companies in industry and transport, 'commercial companies' (banking, insurance, etc.) and the public corporations that administer nationalised industries. As at the end of 1974 the distribution was as follows:—

Companies: *Industrial*		10 234
Commercial		425
Public Sector Members		16
Employers' Organisations and Trade Associations		172
Commercial Associations		31

Two improvements occur from this constitution over that of the old confederation; both large unfederated firms, such as Ford and Vauxhall, and employers from the public sector are included. Under this arrangement the CBI in total covers about three-quarters of all employers in the UK, and so is highly representative from the industrial relations point of view.

Government

The CBI is governed by a very large council with more than four hundred members. Activities are largely divided, however, amongst a large number of committees. Even so, those that are concerned with labour relations can be very large with over a hundred members. Such large numbers indicate the concern of the various employers' organisations and associations included in the CBI to be directly represented.

A point made at the outset is worth repeating in this context, which is that the CBI only moves on a consensus of opinion. In fact, it can only advise; it cannot intervene. CBI powers in this respect are more limited than those of the TUC which can intervene in serious industrial disputes.

Departments and Committees

The CBI is organised into eight departments under the overall control of a Director-General. This figure is analagous to the TUC's General Secretary, and he usually acts as the CBI's spokesman. Each department has its own full-time staff under a director, and services a number of standing committees (another paralled with the TUC). The list of these departments serves to indicate the overall scope of the CBI's activities: Economic, Company Affairs, Regional and Smaller Firms; Information; Administration; Education, Training and Technology; Overseas; and Social Affairs. It is the last mentioned with which we are mainly concerned, and this covers a number of important standing committees: Employment Policy; Industrial Relations and Manpower; International Labour; Labour and Social Affairs; Safety, Health and Welfare; Social Security; and Wages and Conditions.

Regional and overseas offices

Unlike the TUC, the CBI has a number of regional offices in the UK and one at Brussels to deal with immediate EEC problems. Within the UK these offices act as centres for Regional Councils.

Present-day style and functions

In its hand-out to prospective members the CBI claims that it is 'a non-political organisation, formed by British business to safeguard the interests of industry and commerce at Westminister, Whitehall, the Regions, Brussels and wherever decisions are taken which affect the business community. For that community the CBI performs the roles of spokesman, top level negotiator, advisor, forward planner, and "general staff".' The claim to be non-political means that like the TUC it is not affiliated to any political party. But it should not be taken to mean that the CBI does not become involved in political issues.

In his 1974 Annual Report, the President regretted that 'the CBI was drawn much further into the political arena than most of us would normally have wished. Although the CBI is not party political, it certainly has a duty to explain and defend the responsible free enterprise system when this system is challenged and attacked. Various elements in the Government's industrial, employment and fiscal proposals, as presented, would have undermined the free enterprise system and appeared to be quite contrary to the Government's stated desire to ensure a vigorous and profitable private sector'. In particular the CBI were opposed to nationalisation plans, the Employment Protection Bill, and the Wealth and Capital Transfer Tax proposals. Some sections of the White Paper, 'Regeneration of British Industry' also met with their disapproval.

Given its concern to maintain a profitable private sector, the CBI is bound on occasion to oppose the socialist policies of Labour Governments. The CBI is still vigorously opposed to plans for the state take-over of shipbuilding and docks and harbours. Quite a campaign was mounted against extensions of public ownership and a number of publications were widely distributed. More generally, the CBI looks critically at Government intervention in industry. A major document, 'Industry and Government', alleged that existing state controls were hampering industry and stressed the need for Government to allow free enterprise to respond more effectively to market forces.

Although the CBI may not be party political in their constitution, they are not above becoming involved as the occasion seems to merit. Quoting again from the 1974 Annual Report, this time with regard to the Trade Union and Labour Relations Act, 'the CBI co-operated closely with opposition MPs; significant changes, many proposed or supported by the CBI, were made during the late parliamentary stages.'

The special understanding between the present Labour Government and the TUC, the 'Social Contract', helps to explain why the CBI has in fact become quite so overtly involved in party politics. There is nothing novel, however, about the CBI's lack of sympathy with socialist policies.

The CBI has inherited from the old Confederation, a concern for 'management's right to manage'. This partly accounts for their opposition to the Employment Protection

Act, and it is clearly evident in the cool reception they have given to Common Market proposals on participation. Another document entitled 'Employee Participation' rejected the mandatory two-tier board system and was generally opposed to legislation on this subject, which they thought should be treated on a company-by-company basis. Even here they only envisage better communications and consultation, which, as will become apparent in the relevant chapter of this book, are scarcely to the point.

If the state, particularly under Labour, has drawn the CBI albeit unwillingly into party politics, it has also drawn that organisation more into partnership with the TUC through a number of Government agencies. The case of the National Economic Development Council has already been mentioned. The CBI is also represented along with the TUC on the Manpower Commission, the Advisory, Conciliation and Arbitration Service, and the Health and Safety Commission. The pattern already observed, of the CBI, like the old Confederation, being prompted by the Government into greater co-operation with the TUC, still continues.

FURTHER READING

TUC Disputes Principles and Procedures (TUC, 1976)
ABC of TUC (TUC, 1975)
A Short History of the TUC, J. Lovell and B. C. Roberts (Macmillan, 1968)

QUESTIONS FOR DISCUSSION

1 Ought Trades Union Congress to have more control of member-unions, and if so in what ways?
2 Can the CBI and TUC genuinely avoid becoming involved in party politics?

6

International Organisation

Modern capitalism has been international in character from its origins. It was access to world markets which provided the stimulus for Britain's industrial revolution. A reliance on imported raw materials is just as old; the cotton industry drew its raw materials from the southern United States. As the new methods of manufacture spread through Europe in the nineteenth century, socialists asserted that the proletariat had no nationality, that capitalism had broken down such barriers. They were to be sadly disappointed at the outbreak of the First World War. The 'First International' was formed in 1868 and included a number of prominent British trade unionists (The International Working Men's Association), but it cannot be said that this had very much bearing on their trade union activities. The 'First International' was not in fact a trade union organisation as such and included a wide variety of political opinions.

The sheer size and influence of modern multi-national companies has reminded trade unions of the need for some effective form of international organisation. Since the 1950s these companies have been investing heavily in manufacturing industry in industrial countries. The TUC Economic Review for 1975 noted that of the hundred largest economic units in the world, fewer than half were nation states, and that many multi-nationals had a turn-over which was larger than the gross national product of a medium-sized industrial country. Many British companies are subsidiaries of multi-nationals. Over three thousand British companies are owned and controlled from abroad. Some British-based companies are multi-nationals: ICI produce about three-quarters as much abroad as they do in this country. In addition there are bi-nationals such as Unilever and Shell, which are both Anglo-Dutch.

International capital movements are not new. Exports of capital from Britain were on a fairly massive scale from the 1870s. The novelty is that unions find themselves negotiating with an employer who is not tied to this country. The employer may threaten to invest elsewhere as a bargaining counter. Both Ford in 1971 and Chrysler in 1973 threatened to cut down their investment in Britain unless they could see an improvement in industrial relations.

Another difficulty occurs with 'transfer pricing'. These are the prices which one subsidiary charges another belonging to the same multi-national company. These prices are fixed by head office and effectively allow the company to decide in which country it will take its profits. A subsidiary alleged to be running at a loss may only be doing so because its products to an overseas subsidiary are under-priced. The trade union finds itself in a false position when it comes to negotiate higher wages. Transfer pricing is very difficult if not impossible to prove from published accounts. The TUC has estimated that 25% of UK exports are sales between sectors of multi-national companies (TUC *Economic Review*, 1976).

The size of the problem seems to be more obvious than the remedies. Usually the TUC presses the government to exercise some sort of control. International organisation on the part of trade unions to match that of the multi-nationals seems to be called for, but there is very little progress in this direction. Bearing in mind the world-wide span and power of these multi-nationals, it is a rather daunting prospect. The TUC perseveres with existing organisations.

The International Labour Organisation (ILO)

The ILO is all that remains of the League of Nations which

followed the First World War. Set up under the Treaty of Versailles in 1919, it survived to become a specialised agency of the United Nations in 1946. Its fundamental aim is to promote social justice throughout the world by establishing humane conditions of labour. This objective is pursued in three ways:

(a) International standards are formulated as Conventions, Recommendations, and Resolutions.

(b) Information, including statistics, is collected and distributed.

(c) Technical assistance is given to member states.

Conventions, Recommendations and Resolutions

The International Labour Conference, which meets annually, has representatives from the governments, employers and workers of each member state. In Britain the CBI and TUC supply employer and worker representatives respectively. This conference, therefore, forms an international forum for the discussion of all industrial relations matters. These discussions can lead to Conventions, Recommendations or Resolutions, and the differences are important.

Conventions require a two-thirds majority and are then similar to international treaties. Each member state is bound to submit a convention to the appropriate authority, Parliament in our case. If a member state accepts a convention, it is said to be 'ratified', and that state is obliged to bring its practice and laws into line with the convention. However, member states are not obliged to comply with conventions they have not ratified. Britain has ratified two conventions that are of the first importance to trade unions.

Convention No. 87, concerning Freedom of Association and Protection of the Right to Organise states that:

'. . . workers' and employers' organisations shall have the right to draw up their constitutions and rules, to elect their representatives in full freedom, to organise their administration and activities and to formulate their programmes—public authorities shall refrain from any interference which would restrict this right or impede the lawful exercise thereof.'

British governments have, to say the least, given this convention a rather liberal interpretation at times, as we shall see later in this book.

Convention No. 98, concerning the Application of the Principles of the Right to Organise and to Bargain Collectively provides that:

'... workers shall enjoy adequate protection against acts of anti-union discrimination in respect of their employment' which applies particularly to any attempt to 'make the employment of a worker subject to the conditions that he shall not join a union or shall relinquish trade union membership' or to 'cause the dismissal of or otherwise prejudice a worker by reason of union membership or because of participation in union activities.'

An interesting point here is that British enactment took place in the early seventies whereas the Convention was adopted by the ILO in 1949.

Some Conventions cover matters which in Britain are the subject of voluntary collective bargaining. Traditionally our government did not intervene in this area so that it was not normally able to ratify them. The situation today is rather complex so far as the British government's role is concerned, and it requires the rather lengthy explanation given in Chapter 12. But, as an example, equal pay for women was adopted by the ILO for many years before our government decided that such a matter was their concern. This difficulty does not arise where there is statutory wage regulation, as under Wages Councils or Boards.

Recommendations must also be submitted to Parliament but they do not call for ratification. Two adopted in 1951 lay down general principles for collective bargaining and the voluntary settlement of disputes. Resolutions express the opinion of conference but involve no obligations on member states.

The International Labour Office

This has its headquarters in Geneva and branches throughout the world, including one in London (87–91 New Bond Street, W1). Having the same initials as the Organisation it can be confused with that body, but the International Labour *Office* is the executive branch.

It provides the full-time secretariat, organises conferences and meetings, collects information and does research, and administers technical aid schemes. Unions and management obtain a number of useful publications from this source, particularly as regards certain standards. Work study engineers make use of their standards on relaxation allowances or on lighting. Union negotiators refer to the same source especially on questions of health and safety. Very often there is no British standard to refer to in this field. The office is also an important provider of statistical information. The Department of Employment Gazette reproduces their statistics on stoppages in various countries.

International trade union organisation

Formal world-wide federations of trade unions have a long if not very successful history. In 1901, largely at the instigation of German trade unions, the International Federation of Trade Unions was formed. Prior to the First World War, French unions pressed the IFTU to declare an international general strike to prevent any outbreak of hostilities. The IFTU thought the question was outside its province and referred it to the International Socialist Congress. In the event, workers in the various countries rallied to their national colours and the IFTU disappeared. Even leaders of the CGT in France gave their support to the war in the name of 'sacred unity'. The secretary of the Metalworkers' Federation said: 'At that moment, the working class would not have left it to the police to shoot us; they would have shot us themselves.' [1] In 1919 the IFTU was revived but came into immediate conflict with the 'Red International of Labour Unions' organised by the new Communist government in Russia.

Between the wars, national differences combined with ideological disputes to weaken any resolution there might have been in the face of a world slump and the rise of national socialism. Free trade unions were brutally suppressed in Germany, Italy and Spain. By 1939 there was no world-wide organisation to speak of. Immediately after the war a conference was called in London at which a new organisation was created, the World Federation of Trade Unions. Prime movers of this development were the union organisations of the USA, Britain and Russia. As the Cold War set in, ideological differences deepened and the refusal of the Communist block to have anything to do with Marshall Aid was the occasion for Western trade unions to withdraw from the WFTU.

In 1949 another conference was called in London by non-Communist federations and they formed their own International Confederation of Free Trade Unions (ICFTU). This is the world organisation to which the TUC is still affiliated and it covers nearly 60 million workers in over a hundred countries. By definition this organisation stands for the defence and encouragement of trade unions which are independent of the state. That allows a wide spread of ideas on the basic role of trade unions and their relations with political parties and the Church. The ICFTU is then a loose alliance, and as we shall see affiliation to it can mean different things in different countries.

Meanwhile the WFTU continues to be completely dominated by Communists. The great bulk of its membership comes from within the Soviet block, although it has important Communist affiliates in France and Italy. In the past the WFTU has adhered strictly to the Communist

---

[1] See *The Trade Union Movement in France*, p. 2, EEC Press & Information, 1972.

Party line, but now that the French and Italian Communist parties have declared their independence of Soviet policy, there may be a different set of implications. Since both these countries are members of the Common Market there could be important consequences for trade union unity within that area.

The third world-wide organisation, though much smaller than the other two, is the World Confederation of Labour (WCL). Originally this was formed from specifically Catholic unions and was called the International Federation of Christian Trade Unions (IFTCU—not to be confused with the ICFTU). Following the papal encyclical, 'Rerum Novarum' of 1891, which condemned the class struggle and attacks on the notion of private property associated with socialistic unions, Catholic workers were encouraged to form their own organisations. On the mainland of Europe in countries with a substantial population of Catholic workers, there arose these specifically Catholic unions.

The situation is more complicated today. From about 1950, these unions were busy recruiting in French overseas possessions. They obtained a substantial number of Muslims in Algeria and of Buddhists in Vietnam. For a long time the test of membership was that the applicant was *'croyant'*, that is, had some belief in the supernatural. The term 'Christian' clearly became a misnomer. At the same time these organisations felt that they might recruit workers within Europe who, although not Christians, shared the 'Christian social ethic'. The name was changed, therefore, to that of the World Confederation of Labour.

In France the *Confédération Française Démocratique du Travail* (CFDT)—The French Democratic Federation of Labour—has distanced itself still further from the Church, and now advocates a movement towards a democratic socialist society, although remaining a member of the WCL. Another French union, *'Force Ouvrière'* (FO) is an ICFTU member and this is in competition with the CFDT. Force Ouvrière, in fact, follows the French syndicalist tradition which is committed to complete independence of all political parties. Just to underline the point made earlier that affiliation to the ICFTU means different things in different countries, it may be noted that the Italian Catholic organisation (CISL) is a member of the ICFTU.

This tripartite division of unions does not apply within every country. In Britain there is one national federation, the TUC, which belongs to the ICFTU, regardless of how many Communists or Catholics are in membership. About half of Germany's population is Catholic, but industry is dominated by the *Deutsche Gewerkschaftsbund* (DGB) — the German Trade Union Federation—with over six million members in affiliated unions; this again is an ICFTU member. North American unions and federations, if they affiliate at all, belong to the same organisation. The general tendency is for national federations rather than individual unions to join a world organisation, although there are some exceptions. Individual unions, therefore, tend to go along with the national federation to which they belong.

Informally a very different picture emerges. Within Holland there is a great deal of co-operation between Catholic and Socialist unions which appear to be moving towards a merger. Some British union leaders pay frequent visits to the Soviet Union and observers from that country are at nearly every Trades Union Congress. There is undoubtedly an international conscience within the trade union movement which fails to find an adequate formal expression, but which upon occasion has important consequences. In recent years British unions have supported Californian grape-pickers and workers in the General Electric Company of America. German workers supported British workers in dispute with Ford. International co-operation can be potent upon a specific issue. General agreement on policies and objectives is not sufficient to make any of these world organisations very significant to practical industrial relations, but one should not assume that trade unions are, therefore, parochial in their outlook.

Europe and the Common Market

The European Trade Union Confederation (ETUC) was formed in 1973 when Britain joined the Common Market. The founding members were OGB—Austria, FGTB—Belgium, LO—Denmark, SAK—Finland, TOC—Finland, FO—France, DGB—Germany, TUC—Britain, AI—Iceland, CISL—Italy, UIL—Italy, CGT—Luxembourg, NVV—Netherlands, LO—Norway, LO—Sweden, TCO—Sweden, SGB—Switzerland and the UGT of Spain. All of these founding members are affiliated to the ICFTU, though not all are from Common Market countries (Austria, Finland, Iceland, Norway, Sweden and Spain are outside the EEC). Ireland was then in the Common Market, but the Irish Congress of Trade Unions did not join the ETUC until March 1974.

Economic integration not only in the Common Market but throughout Europe was part of the reasoning behind such an organisation. Since many of the giant multinational companies also cover North America it would have made good industrial sense to have a formal tie-up with the ICFTU to which all members of the ETUC belong and which covers that continent. A firm alliance on these lines might have made it easier for unions to present an effective countervailing power to the multi-nationals. Such a connection was not possible because within Europe it was important to leave the door open at least to WCL unions and possibly to the Communist unions, should they alter their attitude. Bearing in mind what has been said about the importance of informal arrangements and the close ties which exist between North American unions and those of Western Europe, particularly the British, the pragmatic approach which the ETUC has decided to adopt may prove sufficient. That, however, is looking some way into the future. At present it cannot be said that the giant multi-nationals have much to fear from international union organisation.

Although the ETUC covers a wider area, there is no

doubt that the EEC constitution which provides for extensive consultation with unions was another reason for the formation of the ETUC. A co-ordinated approach to Common Market proposals must enhance the power and influence of trade unions. The following notes indicate the extent of trade union involvement in the running of the EEC.

Economic and Social Committee

The executive body of the Common Market, the Commission, issues proposals which are put to the major consultative bodies, the European Parliament and the above mentioned committee. Trade unions, employers' organisations, and a miscellaneous group known as 'other interests' each have one third of the 144 seats on this committee. Their opinions are passed on with the proposals for the Council of Ministers to make a decision.

Each member state submits to the Council twice as many nominations as it has allotted seats. From each list the council appoints that country's representatives. The allocation of seats is as follows:

Belgium	12
Denmark	9
Germany	24
France	24
Ireland	9
Italy	24
Luxembourg	6
Netherlands	12
United Kingdom	24
	144

Consultative committee for coal and steel

This is a parallel body to that mentioned above dealing specifically with the two industrial sectors mentioned. It has 81 members appointed by the Council on the proposals of the various governments. Trade unions, employers and users are represented.

Standing committee on employment

This committee is composed of 18 trade union and 18 employer representatives appointed by their own organisations, plus an appropriate minister from each of the member states and the member of the European Commission responsible for social affairs.

Trade unions campaigned for the establishment of this committee in 1970. They felt that more emphasis should be placed on employment questions and that face-to-face meetings with ministers would give better results. The Commission stated in their report on European Union, published in July 1975, that they wished to see the role of this committee strengthened as in their view it is 'essential that the two sides of industry should be more closely involved in the preparation of decisions on social and economic issues.'

Those three committees are the most important and those that the reader is most likely to come across in the news. There is, however, a wide variety of other advisory committees on which unions are represented, which deal with particular subjects such as vocational training and health, or with particular industries such as agriculture or transport. In addition there are two institutes with trade union representatives on their management boards; these are the European Centre for Vocational Training located in West Berlin, and the European Foundation for the Improvement of Living and Working Conditions, which is in Ireland. A third institute is to be established in trade union studies, and talks are going on between the Commission and the ETUC.

FURTHER READING

The International Labor Movement by Lewis Lorwin (Greenwood, 1973). In addition the EEC maintains a Trade Union Information Division which issues a number of excellent free publications. They have offices in London,

Edinburgh, Cardiff and Dublin as well as in Washington and New York.

QUESTIONS FOR DISCUSSION

1 What are the obstacles to trade unions forming an effective countervailing power to that of multi-national companies?

2 How might the ETUC wish to see its representation improved within Common Market institutions?

7

The Role of Management

Not so many years ago it would have seemed strange to see management as a group apart from employers. There are still some family firms where some of the owners take an active part in running the business. Larger firms have usually outgrown this idea and tend to employ professional managers. Increasingly there has been, to use a well-worn phrase, a divorce of ownership from control. Managers themselves are now being organised into trade unions, although the process has a long way to go. The British Institute of Management, not a union but a professional association is already asking for separate consultations with the government. There are times, therefore, when it is essential to distinguish between employers and managers. To do so on every occasion would be pedantic, because it is normally management which sits across the table from trade unions arguing on behalf of employers. The major question is: what difference has been made to industrial relations by this divorce of ownership from control? The answer will not be apparent until we know a little more about the structure and techniques of modern management.

Structure of management

A board of directors represents shareholders interests. Once a year they must account to a general meeting of shareholders for their running of the firm. Some of these directors only make their contributions at board meetings, perhaps held once a month. One of their number, however, is designated the 'managing director', and, as his title indicates, he is the head of the firm's management team. There may be other 'executive' directors, such as a sales or technical director, who are also responsible for the day-to-day execution of the board's policies. The board may be roughly compared with a nation's legislature, and management with the executive arm or civil service, so that some directors have a dual function, just as indeed cabinet ministers do. 'Senior management' is not a well-defined term, but it undoubtedly includes those with a share in policy-making.

A 'line manager' is one concerned with an area of production. Usually he has a technical background or has been 'brought up with the firm'. Line managers are generalists in the sense that any problem—technical, commercial or labour—is a possible hindrance to production that they must try to overcome. Supervisors or 'foremen' are the bottom level of line management (sometimes they are called 'first line managers'), and that rank may have its divisions. Above supervisors there is a wider range of ranks referred to as 'middle management'. There is no common terminology but 'works manager' is a title that occurs most frequently. 'General managers' are usually senior works managers.

As you might expect, the responsibilities and status of supervisors, works managers or general managers vary enormously between different firms. A foreman in one firm might have responsibilities equivalent to those of a works manager in another; general managers may be classed as senior or middle management. The organisation pattern, though, is nearly always the same. Proceeding up through the grades there are larger areas of responsibility, a number of supervisors to a works manager and a number of works managers to a general manager, so that they form a pyramid on the organisation chart with the managing director on top.

Some firms only have this line management type of organisation. The development of more sophisticated management techniques, however, has called for specialists known as 'functional management'. Functional managers cover subjects rather than areas of production. A personnel manager will be responsible for personnel matters throughout the plant. There may also be an industrial relations manager. These do not form part of the same neat pyramid and to some extent their duties must overlap with those of line management. Difficulties or even conflicts can occur and these affect industrial relations within the firm.

Line managers have the advantage that they meet workers frequently in unstressed situations. Specialists such as an industrial relations manager may only be called in when there is trouble. Perhaps for that reason some line managers think they are better at industrial relations than the experts. In quite a number of instances they are probably right. The great secret is for the line manager to know just when to hand over to the appropriate specialist.

Procedural agreements attempt to keep the lines of communication clear. An individual with a grievance must first take it to his or her supervisor; if there is failure to agree, then the case goes to a higher level and at some stage a personnel or industrial relations manager is called in. But group grievances normally begin through procedure over the supervisor's head, so that he is left out of the picture. Even higher line management may be left in the dark if negotiations are always conducted with a specialist manager. The communications system develops a short circuit. Theoretically this should not happen, but it does.

Shop stewards are not always happy about dealing with middle management of either type since they do not perhaps have sufficient powers. In that case senior management may come to conduct the bulk of negotiations. The result of this may be to remove most of management from the field of industrial relations. Faced with this type of situation, larger firms have appointed industrial relations directors who attempt to keep settlements in line with the firm's overall policy. Lower levels of management may still find it difficult to cope with agreements which have not taken proper account of the detailed needs of production. A failure to integrate collective bargaining solutions with decision-making at all levels is probably at the root of difficulties of many large firms.

A theme of which students should be aware is that management does not contest wage claims as hard as the owners might. The theory is that since managers are not shareholders, their income is not directly affected when they give way to a wage claim. It is a good deal nearer the truth to note that it is no part of most managers' duties to contest wage claims at all. That goes straight over their heads to a specialist or senior management or even to the board. The career of a manager who does deal with collective bargaining will depend upon his success in containing union demands. If anything he is probably better at this job than most owners would be simply because he is, after all, a professional. No one is likely to be able to prove the truth of the matter one way or the other. One observation, however, is inescapable: the overall performance of large firms with professional managers has been fairly impressive from the shareholder's point of view; generally speaking, they are a better investment. When big firms fall they make a splash in the news; less obvious are the thousands of small firms that fail every year.

Modern management techniques

Management theory has emerged on almost all aspects of working life but is particularly applied to establishing how a job should be done and how it should be rewarded, and to considering interrelationships between the two and differentials between different work groups. It has also been very concerned with the problems of alienation at work and how this can be overcome and to the question of motivation in general.

Here four areas are considered in detail: work study, other motivational techniques, job evaluation and operations research.

(a) *Work study* There are two parts to work study: method study and work measurement. In plain language method study is concerned with finding a better way of doing a job. Methods can be specified in great detail down to instructing a worker as to which hand to use when picking up a tool. Since, as a matter of fact, work study engineers are a part of management, 'better' has usually been associated with 'faster'. Faster methods increase production, reduce labour costs, and—all other things being equal—put up profits. Workers can, of course, claim a share of the increased revenue. At the same time, this way of going about things must further alienate the worker from his work. He is being told how to do his job.

As might be expected, trade unions respond according to whether their approach is ideological or instrumental. Craftsmen tend to be hostile while general workers tend to accept the opportunity to earn some extra money. On these grounds unions either reject or accept method study. They have not done a great deal to turn this technique to their own advantage by finding safer, more congenial or even less alienating methods of work in other respects. The basic principles could be applied to such ends, and it is not true to suggest that there is just one correct method dictated by the need for greater production.

Work measurement is defined by the British Standards Institution as 'the application of techniques designed to establish the time for a qualified worker to carry out a specified job at a defined level of performance'. It may be used entirely for purposes of planning and control or related to financial incentive schemes, and it is the latter application which has more effect on industrial relations.

A qualified worker is one with the capacity to do a particular job. Digging trenches requires a fairly strong person, so that someone qualified to pack chocolates would not necessarily be qualified to dig trenches. With such simple tasks it is no great problem to sort out the capacities required. Within the ranks of qualified workers there will be variations. Two workers putting in the same amount of effort at the same job will perform at different levels, because one is a little stronger or taller or younger. That presents no problem to the philosophy behind financial incentives. The worker who performs better will be paid more and *all* workers will be encouraged to work harder. At this stage in the work study argument there is no attempt to equalise earnings according to the effort which is put in by individuals; it is performance which is measured and rewarded. Later, as we shall see, the idea of rewarding effort creeps back in.

A closely-knit group could already be offended by the ethics behind such a scheme. They may, for example, think it is wrong for their fellow tradesmen to earn less as they grow older. Remember that craft unions originally had an important function as Friendly Societies. The idea that the strong should protect the weak is still an important part of trade union morality. Staunch trade unionists are suspicious of any management technique that may be at all divisive.

But work-measured incentive schemes have advantages for workers over a simple system of payment by results. If a worker accepts financial incentives, he could reasonably expect to earn the same amount whatever job he is given, within his qualifications, provided that he puts in as much effort. It is nothing to do with him if the machine he is operating is more or less efficient. The results, that is, the output, will vary even though his efforts remain the same. Essentially, work-studied incentives claim to reward 'performance' regardless of factors outside the worker. To the extent that this is true, they offer a more equitable payment system than one based entirely on results.

The claim of work study engineers to be able to measure performance accurately regardless of outside factors is disputed. The more complex and varied that jobs are, the more room there is for argument. What happens then is that shop stewards will be found negotiating with work study engineers, particularly over 'allowances' for excessive heat or cold or what-have-you. The immediate effect upon industrial relations is that there is a shift of power towards shop stewards. When a scheme has 'decayed', earnings may be virtually under the control of shop stewards. An important factor here is the number of 'bargaining opportunities' that stewards are afforded from job changes. Many other factors have a bearing, including the strength of union organisation, the number of competing unions, the state of the labour market, and so on. The point is that work measurement is not nearly so objective as is sometimes claimed, at least not in practice. Changing a firm's payment system can radically alter 'factory politics' as it grants more or less power to shop stewards.

There have been price lists, that is, prices for completed operations, since the early nineteenth century. Coal miners used to be paid on a sliding scale. They were paid according to how many tons of coal they brought up, but their earnings were adjusted according to the current price of coal. Modern work study techniques are not based on the price of the product. It does not matter whether output fetches more or less in the market. There is a qualitative difference between dealing with this type of management and dealing with the owners of a business. A degree of specialisation moves work-study engineers at least one stage from the market place. They probably know less about a firm's profits in many instances than do the shop stewards they are dealing with.

(*b*) *Other motivational techniques* Ask most people why they go to work, and they will say for the money. Most people would not carry on working at their job, could not in fact, unless they were paid. Money is a *necessary* condition for them to stay at their present job. It is not, however, a *sufficient* condition, because there are other jobs that they would not do for the same or even higher pay. A given wage does not finally decide which employment we take up. Motivational theory is concerned with the whole range of reasons that people have for remaining in a particular employment and working conscientiously.

There are a number of theories, none of which need detain us beyond noting that the more modern ones call for a more 'participatory' style of management. Employees are made to feel a part of the organisation they work for, to share the corporate goals of the enterprise. Before modern terms were invented, we would have said that the aim was to overcome the alienating nature of industrialised work. The assumption is that the more employees know about their employer's objectives, the more happily they will work. Managers are enjoined to explain what they are doing, and to have more trust in the willingness of workers to co-operate with them.

With regard to our opening question, we have to note a shift away from the cash nexus, at least in managerial theory. Workers are no longer seen as being motivated simply by wages. This is a development of some significance. The arguments of such theories and the results of some experiments, particularly in the United States, provide a lot of ammunition for those who advocate a higher degree of workers' control. When both are advocating more industrial democracy, it is difficult to see management and trade unions as being on opposing sides.

A variety of techniques offer ways to overcome the more alienating aspects of detailed work. Job rotation means moving workers round to break some of the monotony. Job enlargement goes against the principle of division of labour and seeks to give each worker a more meaningful task. 'Job enrichment' is a term which refers to groups of workers being allowed to supervise themselves. It is significant that management has taken these initiatives. No doubt they are aimed at maintaining a stable and contented workforce. Full employment with labour shortages and the needs of better-educated workers have probably occasioned their adoption. But they have not resulted from negotiations between 'the two sides of industry'. Management as a separate factor has been principally responsible for these innovations, which have a direct bearing on the state of industrial relations.

(*c*) *Job evaluation* Job evaluation schemes try to fix 'fair' differentials between the earnings of different occupations. How much, for example, should a tool-setter, any tool-setter, be paid as compared to a crane-driver? That is the sort of question they try to answer. Job evaluation is not concerned with the performance of one tool-setter as against another. There are a number of different schemes but they all aim at the same objective, which is to remove any sense of injustice about differentials. The more sophisticated types take a number of 'factors'—physical effort, training, working conditions, and so on. Each factor is then given a weighting or so many maximum points. The idea then is that a job can be given a monetary value according to the number of points it scores. As any schoolboy knows, you cannot add up apples and pears; and no more can you add up mental and physical effort. There is no scientific measurement that covers all types of human endeavour. Job evaluation has at some stage to make subjective judgements. What weighting will be given to so many years' training? What weighting will be given to working in unpleasant conditions? These judgements will be valid if they represent a consensus of opinion, because then they will be 'fair'. This, after all, is the ultimate objective. Getting that consensus requires the co-operation of all the workers concerned. Differentials are fair when, and only when, the workers concerned think they are.

Job evaluation cuts into traditional collective bargaining. Differentials have been fixed largely by the relative bargaining power of different groups. On this count more powerful groups may be unwilling to accept job evaluation schemes. Secondly, trade unions apart, supply and demand for a type of labour must affect its price. If there is an acute shortage of electricians, their wages can be expected to rise. These difficulties do not prevent job evaluation schemes being installed in some places quite successfully.

Management in any case are not concerned to favour one group of workers more than another. Their interest is in avoiding friction between different groups or trades. Obviously, that is in the long-run interest of the firm, but it is not the same as management siding with employers against employees. Management are in a neutral position.

(*d*) *Operations research* There is a range of quantitative techniques which are grouped together under the title of operations research. They have the effect of replacing judgement based upon experience with precise quantitative techniques which give correct solutions to managerial problems. This type of decision-making is less easily challenged by the union or anyone else. An old-style manager faced with the problem of how many cash points to have in a store might scratch his head and, using his judgement and experience, come up with a number. No doubt good managers are usually right and the latest techniques would provide the same answer. But a trade union representative might match his judgement and experience against that of a manager. He might say that he has worked in the store for as long as the manager and that when he scratched his head a different number came to mind. Modern-style management would use 'queueing theory' to solve this type of problem, and, if their decision were challenged by anyone, simply present their statistical working. Suppose that the trade union representative is familiar with this technique; he might possibly find a mistake in the statistics, but he is not likely to detect any managerial bias.

Objective decision-making can scarcely be described as representing the employer's interests any more than any other job in the establishment. The manager is only doing a job like any other employee and if that is said to be in the employer's interests, which employee is to cast the first stone? The 'two sides of industry' are not so clearly drawn.

Our question at the beginning of the chapter was whether the divorce of ownership from control had had much effect on industrial relations. The answer, it was suggested, lay in the structure and techniques of modern management. What we have seen is that a more professional style of management has accompanied the economic trend towards larger firms. Increasing professionalism has tended to shift the line manager, the generalist, away from the area of collective bargaining. As a result some agreements may not be compatible with production requirements at lower levels. Whether this means that modern management is any softer than owner-proprietors would be is a moot point. Professional industrial relations managers may not be so acutely aware of production requirements, but they are likely to be more highly skilled negotiators.

If we allow that management are primarily the employers' agents, we must admit that they have made the 'game' of collective bargaining a much more sophisticated one. The more objective or at least systematic that management becomes, the less obvious it is that it is acting chiefly in the owners' interests. Value judgements about ultimate aims may lie deep beneath some techniques, and neither management nor unions be aware of a built-in bias. Method study at present comes into this category, although it need not necessarily do so.

Some techniques go further than that and place management in an entirely neutral position. What value judgements there are can be left to the workforce, as with a well-conducted job evaluation scheme.

When we look into those motivational techniques which seek to overcome the alienating nature of industrial work, management appear on the same side as the trade unions. Management are directly tackling the type of problem which first called modern trade unionism into existence. This is a much more complicated question, however, and one that we shall return to in the final chapter, after we have considered participation and industrial democracy in more depth in Chapter 12.

FURTHER READING

There is a useful chapter in Hugh Clegg's *System of Industrial Relations in Great Britain*.

The TUC issue a series of pamphlets on Job Evaluation, Work Study and Profits. Management students will already be aware of more advanced texts.

QUESTIONS FOR DISCUSSION

1 Suppose that there were no private firms and that there was no profit motive; what role would management have?
2 Ought the government to consult the BIM as well as the TUC and the CBI?

8

The Role of Shop Stewards

Shop stewards are trade union representatives at the work-place. With very few exceptions they are elected by members of a particular union in their section of the firm or 'shop', for example the paint shop, warehouse or tool room. After election most of them carry on with the work for which they were originally employed, and they are still paid by their firm and not by the union.

The actual term 'shop steward' is most common in manu-facturing industry but similar representatives exist under a variety of names in other sectors. There are two major difficulties in the way of any detailed description of their function. Firstly, there is an enormous diversity between the roles of stewards in different firms or unions. It would be surprising if this were not the case, bearing in mind the number of unions involved with thousands of firms in all sorts of industries. Any attempt to standardise this representation would probably prove disastrous. The only common factor is that, officially, a steward is supposed to be a link man between members on the shop floor and the union's full-time officials. A second and connected difficulty arises from the fact that we are dealing with a very informal institution. Union rule books and Shop Stewards' Handbooks—issued to them by their union if at all—form a poor guide to what it is that stewards actually do. There is more to this, however, than the mere technical difficulties of dealing with such a varied function. An outline of the history of the shop steward movement is necessary to understand the extension of its influence far beyond official limits and the reluctance of unions to bring their rules into line with established fact.

Throughout the nineteenth century we can find evidence of spokesmen at the workplace who were not full-time officials. But it was not until the First World War that shop stewards, largely within the munitions industries, became a powerful national force. Lloyd George as Minister for Munitions referred to the hostilities as a 'war of engineers'. He meant that victory depended upon the efficient organisation of industry because of the vast amount of armaments and ammunition needed to fight a modern war. The British engineering industry had undergone considerable changes but they were not so revolutionary as to sweep away the craft tradition. When new methods had been introduced skilled men had succeeded in 'following the machine', so that they still dominated in the workforce. On the shop floor these artisans maintained a considerable degree of control and the major lock-outs by employers in the nineteenth century were about the 'power to manage'. Those confrontations occurred between the employers and the union led by its national officials. A number of factors led to a split in the First World War between union officialdom and the men on the shop floor. A massive expansion and technical re-organisation of the industry was necessary to provide all the arms and ammunition needed to fight a modern war. The government was compelled to intervene not only to allow new machinery and unskilled workers into the industry, but also to direct skilled labour. Although the government was able to win the co-operation of national officials through the famous Treasury Agreements, men on the shop floor did not feel they had been fairly treated and the Shop Stewards Movement arose.

History does teach some lessons and this is one that ought not to go unnoticed: you cannot cut off the head of the trade union movement. Had this fact been realised the Industrial Relations Act of 1971 would have been drafted very differently. Rank and file members do not simply take orders

from their officials and they regard them more as their servants than their masters.

What the government and employers in fact sought was
the co-operation of the workforce. In practice this had to be
obtained by detailed negotiations with shop stewards. It
was not simply the workers' rebellion which made this
necessary. We can sum up the other factors by saying that
they all pointed to the need for plant rather than national
bargaining. Before the war the typical manufacturing unit
was small and not specialised. As we have seen larger firms
tend to have greater alienation problems and therefore to
require constant worker representation. A full-time official
cannot be in constant attendance at all the firms nominally
under his control. Power inevitably tends to shift towards
the man on the spot: the shop steward. Firms became much
larger through the influx of unskilled workers, many of
them women, referred to significantly as 'dilutees'. Clearly
this expansion required considerable revision of working
rules to decide what work should be allowed to the new
people and at what rates of pay, and so on. Had these
changes been fairly uniform throughout the industry,
national negotiations might still have been realistic. But as
firms tended to specialise they became very different from
one another. In order to cover all this diversity any new set
of rules would have been too complex and too slow to make
up. War required rapid adaptation from established workers
and this could be achieved more easily plant by plant. Apart
from questions of speed and flexibility there is always the
point that the closer people are to any sort of rule-making
the more confident they will feel. The circumstances which
make for in-plant bargaining always favour the shop steward
movement.

Between the wars the situation was pretty well reversed
and as we would expect, shop stewards declined in number
and importance. National agreements became the order of
the day as the union's hierarchy reasserted its authority.
There was a world-wide slump and as a result the industry
contracted and stagnated. With widespread unemployment

the bargaining power of labour diminished, and shop stewards, as employees of their firms, were in a particularly vulnerable position. In any case, without investment in new plant and machinery there was less to negotiate. Falling prices meant that the employers had to cut their labour costs. The necessary wage reductions were put through without any great difficulty on a national basis.

The factors which gave rise to the shop steward movement were restored in the Second World War. Ever since then a scarcity at least of skilled labour, combined with increasing size and specialisation in firms, has favoured plant bargaining and so the need to deal with stewards. Shop floor representatives when compared with full-time officials are rather like the figures on a weather clock: as one side comes into prominence the other withdraws. It now seems, however, as if plant bargaining is here to stay. After more than thirty years, the authority of stewards ought to be given more formal recognition.

One can sympathise with unions' reluctance to make any sweeping changes to their rules, bearing in mind the complexity of a shop steward's role. A steward's function may be seen from a number of angles. The four most important viewpoints are those of the members who elected him, his fellow stewards, his trade union, and his employers, though not necessarily in that order.

Stewards are elected every one or two years, usually by a show of hands on the shop floor from members of a particular union. If there is more than one union, then in most cases there will be a steward for each, although this is not always so. The position is not much sought after since it involves a lot of responsibility with very few benefits if any for the holder.

There is always the risk that in acting as spokesman for grievances the steward may come to be regarded by management as a 'trouble maker'. On the other hand, if members feel that their representative is not pressing their case hard enough, they will criticise him. There is no extra pay for the job. Where workers are paid by results, the best practice is for management to make up earnings for time lost on union business. Some stewards collect subscriptions and are given a small commission by the union, but this rarely provides much incentive. The modern tendency is either for subscriptions to be collected by a special money steward or for the firm to deduct them from wages, using 'the check-off method'. In craft unions members are often expected to take the subscriptions to the branch so that the steward does not become involved at all.

Figure 1

Role of a Shop Steward

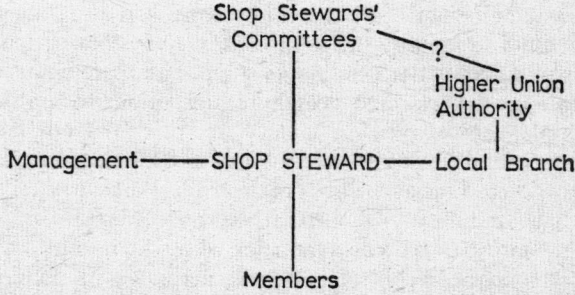

One often hears the tale that election as a steward is the first step on the ladder to promotion within a firm. Certainly stewards are sometimes promoted to become supervisors or even personnel managers. One theory is that management do this to get rid of trouble makers: they promote them out of the way. The truth of the matter would be hard to measure but it is such well-established folk-lore that one suspects there must be some truth in it. It seems just as likely, however, that good stewards jeopardize their normal promotion prospects.

In Chapter 1 we observed that a feature of industrial work was that it was carried out by co-operative groups or teams. Such groups naturally tend to find a spokesman from amongst their number. From the shop floor's point of view the chief function of a steward is to act as their voice. Only a member of the group can adequately fulfill this function, someone who works alongside them and knows exactly how it feels. We might put it that a steward is expected to be of the same mind as his members. When these representatives spend too much time on union business there is often a certain loss of confidence because they are thought to have moved *too far away from the tools*. Even if unions did create enough officials to cover every single plant, there would still be a psychological need for a working group to have this *voice*.

Unfortunately, not enough people are prepared to be nominated, so that the accredited steward frequently has to speak on behalf of a number of groups. It is also difficult sometimes to identify the right constituency, that is, those people or occupations calling for a separate representative. They may be scattered geographically; train drivers, for example, work all over the country, and oddly enough, men on the front of the train (the footplate staff) form a separate group, from those at the back of the train (the guards). The group should ideally be one that feels a close identity of interest, but there is no one yardstick with which to measure this. Economic, technical, historical, perhaps even political or cultural factors may all have a bearing. With all these difficulties and anomalies in mind, it remains axiomatic to nearly every shop steward that he or she should intuitively react to a given situation in the way that his or her members expect.

This relationship is easy to misunderstand. People outside industry often think of a steward as a leader in the sense of a gifted or specially trained person, able to direct or give orders to workers. No doubt some of them have strong personalities; they may be highly articulate, perhaps even 'natural leaders'—whatever that means. Nevertheless, their authority rests four-square upon a close identity with those who elected them. Very little authority if any is vested in them by the union. The power of a steward is determined in the last analysis by the degree of support that he has. If his mind is their mind then the workers will back him all the way. If he is thought to be a shade too clever or devious, that support will be less and less forthcoming. Finally, the shop floor will simply refuse to back a certain course of action. The writer can recall one instance where a steward called out his members in the morning. They returned in the afternoon having elected themselves a fresh shop steward. The informality of the system makes it one of very simple, direct democracy, and this is one good reason for the parties concerned not having any great desire to make it more formal.

All the stewards in a plant may meet together on a shop stewards' committee. If they come from a number of unions, this is called the Joint Shop Stewards' Committee (JSSC). From their number one is elected as a spokesman for the committee. The title of this person varies: sometimes it is simply 'Senior Shop Steward'; in printing it has the rather grand name of 'Imperial Father of the Chapel', but the most common term is 'Convener'. Where there are thought to be fundamental differences of interest between the various unions, there may be more than one such committee, each with its own convener.

For day-to-day industrial relations these committees are vital for co-ordinating the activities of individual stewards. When new rules have to be made which will apply to the whole plant or firm, a uniform agreement has to be reached. Both sides of industry are concerned that the differentials between one group of workers and another should be seen to be fair. Stewards are well aware of the fact that they are likely to obtain a better bargain if they can present a united front: they certainly do not wish to allow management to play one set of workers off against another. Acting on the principle that two heads are better than one, or perhaps suspecting that some fundamental principle may be at stake, a steward will frequently seek the opinions of his colleagues on questions which are entirely his own responsibility. After all, some of those colleagues may have a great deal more experience as shop stewards. Furthermore, some written agreements for the settlement of disputes lay down that the convener will be involved before any action is taken.

These committees, therefore, have become important institutions. Whilst they provide the lone steward with help and advice, they can also give rise to conflicting loyalties. It can happen that the view of the committee, carried by a majority vote, is different from that of a steward's own shop. If the differences are difficult to reconcile, the steward may feel torn between loyalty to the committee and loyalty to his shop, although he knows that in the end it is the latter which must prevail. Any co-ordinating body, however, is a possible source of friction, and most stewards rapidly become good committee men. Next to being a true voice for his own group or groups, this is possibly the most important attribute of a good steward.

Joint Shop Stewards' Committees are not answerable to any single union, although some federations of unions have tried to control them without much success. In theory a union may discipline one of its own stewards and on occasions some have done so. In reality this is not always a practicable proposition, whatever the rule book may say. But in both theory and practice, joint committees of stewards are free to pursue a line in defiance of officially declared policies. The surprising thing is not that this occurs but that it does not occur more frequently.

Recent years have seen the growing importance of Combine or Group Committees which have developed alongside the large, multi-plant companies. Representatives from the various plants around the country meet to formulate common policies. In general this development follows the principle of countervailing power: as firms have grown larger, the stewards' committees have had to cover a wider area. Since this is a move from plant towards national bargaining, it is one that impinges on the authority of the official hierarchy of trade unions in an area they had regarded as their own. Some combine committees issue their own newspapers and the public media have given considerable publicity to their views on major disputes. These organisations form the summit of the shop steward movement.

Relations with official trade union structure

Stewards were first recognised as link men between the branch and the shop floor. Rules tend to perpetuate this attitude. Typically, stewards' duties are seen as encouraging recruitment, collecting subscriptions, and informing members of union policy. Only gradually are unions coming to recognise in their rules the true significance of shop stewards. The EETU, for example, has conferences for stewards by industry at national and regional level. Most unions still appear reluctant to see this movement as initiating union policy.

There is the structural problem. Shop stewards' committees are more rational than the official structure in plant and company terms, except where there is an industrial union. Elsewhere, as mentioned, a joint shop stewards' committee cannot be held answerable to a single union. Federations of unions might have more control, and some have actually issued credentials. At present it cannot be said that any marked degree of integration has been achieved in this way. Individual unions are still jealous of their autonomy, and the CSEU—the most important of official multi-union industrial groups—is composed of different types of union with different outlooks.

There is no easy solution to the problem. In the meantime, the important thing to remember is that stewards perform those functions their unions expect of them, but they also do much more.

Relations with management

Management's viewpoint is pragmatic. They need shop stewards for an accurate impression of their employees' reactions. The larger the undertaking, the more necessary is this channel of communication. If this were not the case it would be hard to explain the encouragement which managers usually give to stewards, even to the extent of paying their wages whilst they go on training courses. In the writer's experience, stewards themselves are not keen to admit that they have any obligation to management, beyond that of any other worker. Yet again this is something which arises inevitably from their position as 'the man in the middle'. First and foremost stewards see themselves as being on the side of the workers. But in conveying the views, feelings or aspirations of those workers, these representatives are performing a service to management. Furthermore, negotiations have to be reported back to the shop floor, giving a two-way channel of communication. Confrontations do arise, perhaps even leading to a strike; but if managers automatically blame their stewards, they are behaving like those ancient despots who executed any messenger who brought them bad news.

In the outline of the history of the movement we noted that plant bargaining had considerable advantages under certain conditions, and that it enhanced the role of stewards in the eyes of management. Managers still show a general preference for dealing with their own employees rather than bringing in a full-time official, although this is not universal. We would not expect it to be true everywhere, bearing in mind the particular circumstances that favour plant bargaining. Under any circumstances, however, there are certain advantages to this approach: the employee is more familiar with the firm, which means that management do not have to spell out all the technical and commercial implications of any new arrangement. Perhaps, more simply, a firm does not wish to wash its dirty linen in public. Just as important is the fact that an employee has a greater commitment to his firm; after all, his job is at stake. It is not right to think of stewards and management as being at perpetual loggerheads. Surveys (given in 'Further Reading') have shown that a working relationship between management and stewards is the norm rather than the exception.

FURTHER READING

Historical:
Workshop Organisation by G. D. H. Cole (reprinted by Hutchinsons in 1973).
The First Shop Stewards Movement by James Hinton (George Allen and Unwin, 1973).

Surveys:
Workplace Industrial Relations, Government Social Survey, 1968.
The Role of Shop Stewards in British Industrial Relations, W. E. J. McCarthy, Royal Commission Research Paper No. 1.
Shop Stewards in British Industry, J. F. B. Goodman and T. G. Whittingham (McGraw-Hill, 1960).

QUESTIONS FOR DISCUSSION

1 Bearing in mind the different types of union that exist, is the informality of the shop steward movement good or bad?
2 Ought shop stewards to be leaders?
3 Is it right for management to have the right as they sometimes do, to approve shop steward's credentials?

Part Two: Collective Bargaining and Participation

So far we have been concerned with the principal parties to industrial relations and we now turn to the ways in which they interact. Apart from national negotiations conducted by industrial unions, which is exceptional in Britain, the workers' side is represented by a combination of union representatives. It is not possible to understand how a 'bargaining unit' is formed without some consideration of those factors which give workers a unity of interest, including the economic realities behind bargaining power. That is the subject of Chapter 9. The following chapter goes on to describe the way that the 'game' of free collective bargaining is played. 'Free' in this sense means free from government intervention; although this is the traditional style of collective bargaining, Chapter 11, on government, shows that present-day practice is very much more complicated. Collective bargaining is only one form taken by the search for more industrial democracy, and Chapter 12 deals with other forms, paying particular attention to participation, since this is of current interest.

9

The Organisation of Bargaining

A phrase often used to sum up all the things which go towards making workers feel that they belong to one group rather than another is 'unity of interests'. When workers have found the right union for them, that body need not be entirely responsible for negotiating their pay and conditions: the case of the NUM, which conducts negotiations on behalf of nearly all employees in the industry, is exceptional. Most unions must divide their efforts. A craft union, say that covering electricians, will have members in nearly every industry. The members they have in engineering will have a different set of requirements from those in the entertainment industry.

When we take each industry, it is obvious that all employees have something in common, but this is not usually enough to remove the need for more than one union. Our electrician has in mind that he may not always work in this particular industry. All the unions with members in an industry come together on occasion. Whether they choose to negotiate one agreement is a different matter, depending on just how much they have in common. When they do, they form one 'bargaining agency' and all the workers under that agreement form one 'bargaining unit'. Manual workers in electricity supply are covered by one agreement signed by a number of unions.

Bargaining is conducted at different levels: plant, firm or industry. National agreements apply to all the workers in one industry nationwide. Some very large firms, such as Ford,

also have 'national' agreements, meaning that they cover all
their plants in Britain. A common error is to assert the
superiority of plant over national bargaining or vice versa:
there are many factors which help to determine the appropriate bargaining unit, and they do not lead to the same
answer in every case. The more important factors are technological change, modern management techniques, productivity bargaining, management organisation, union
policy, employees' bargaining power, closed shops and
union recognition.

Technological change

When an industry is fairly stable, that is, when it is not
radically altering its method of production, there is less
chance of national officials getting out of touch with conditions on the shop floor. The great majority come from the
shop floor and they remain familiar with its problems. Following the principle that a man's opinion is likely to be as
good as his information, one can say that their judgement is
likely to be sound. If changes are fairly uniform throughout
the industry, officials can perhaps still keep abreast of
them. But if there is at the same time increasing specialisation, so that many firms or plants all seem to be taking off
in different directions, then these officials have a much
greater problem. They may become increasingly liable to
errors of judgement. Shop stewards, on the other hand, have
only the conditions in their particular shop to contend with,
and they are much closer to the members. Rapid change
and diversification tend to be accompanied by plant
bargaining.

National and plant bargaining may operate side by side,
as they did in engineering for many years. In that case it
was plant bargaining that effectively fixed terms and conditions, and the national agreement became largely fictional.
Although in this case the two types of bargaining competed
with each other, it is possible for the two systems to be
harmonised, with agreement being reached as to what items
are suitable for settlement at each level. This is the situation

in nationalised industries, and one towards which engineering is moving.

Modern management techniques

There is no need to repeat the explanations given in Chapter 5. You will recall that modern techniques tend to require more co-operation from the workforce. This co-operation is more realistic when it is obtained at plant level. Indeed some of the techniques are almost impossible to apply over a whole industry. Job evaluation, for example, requires a consensus of opinion which is difficult enough to get at times even on a plant basis. The more general tendency to involve employees in corporate objectives requires employees' aspirations to be included in those objectives. Firms have pulled away from employers' organisations in order to formulate a company policy on industrial relations.

Productivity bargaining

It is essential to craft unionism that the union should try to maintain control over working rules, and it is essential to productivity bargaining that those rules should be relaxed. (The next chapter will explain this more fully.) Within a plant it is possible to specify in detail what relaxations will be made. Craft unions can remain assured that they have not in principle surrendered their control over working practices.

On a national scale this problem becomes virtually insoluble in any diversified industry. A national agreement can only lay down guide-lines which are then subject to in-plant negotiation. For example, it may be agreed at national level that there will be trade union 'co-operation with modern management techniques', but on the shop floor this is fairly meaningless. It does not mean that toolmakers will necessarily allow work study engineers into the tool room.

Management organisation

Management at different levels may have more or less responsibility; it has long been recognised that there is no ideal management organisation. Among the factors which call for differing forms of organisation are the technology employed, the product or product mix, and the product markets. Plants within the same company may produce different products using a variety of techniques or producing for a number of separate markets. Local management may be expected to have a high degree of autonomy. They may, as we say, run their own show. Employees of such a company, faced with a variety of management objectives, will find that plant bargaining suits them better.

Union policy

Trade unions in recent years are tending more to accept the fact of shop steward power. As a general rule, giving stewards more authority encourages plant bargaining.

Bargaining power

Perhaps most important of all is the effectiveness of a particular grouping. Individuals or groups have some idea of what they could get if they were to go it alone, and if a bargaining unit does not meet their expectations, it may start to break up. We refer to the pressure which a group is able to mount on their employer as their bargaining power. This concept is not entirely separate from other factors which go to make up a unity of interests. Some groups are more prepared to carry their weaker brethren than others. This, however, has already been discussed in connection with industrial unions in Chapter 1. Suffice it to say that similar considerations apply to bargaining units as to different types of union. Here we must look into the determinants of bargaining power as economic facts.

Demand for labour is a 'derived' demand: if there is no demand for a product there is no demand for the labour to make it—a truth you may find so self-evident that it does not need stating. Certain consequences are not so obvious. Price is one of the main determinants of the quantity of the product demanded. In this context 'demand' refers to the physical quantity of a good—say, so many tons per annum.

Economists observe three ways by which demand may respond to alterations in price, but for our purpose we need only take account of effects upon revenue. 'Unit elasticity' means that revenue does not alter when the price is altered. Demand falls in physical terms when the price is raised, but revenue does not. The public spend the same amount of revenue on this particular good but get less for it. When demand is 'inelastic' revenue increases as the price is raised, even though the physical quantity sold may be less. 'Elastic demand' produces the opposite result. Perhaps the effect upon wages is already apparent: employers faced with inelastic demand for their product are more ready to give way to wage claims; they can raise their prices and so gain the extra revenue needed to meet extra wage costs.

A variety of reasons could have prevented employers from raising prices previously so as to increase their profits; they include Government policy and a liking for having a waiting list for their products. The nationalised industries have had their prices controlled by Governments, and charges have been below what the market would bear. After the war, the motor vehicle industry had long waiting lists for cars. Increasing their prices meant reducing the length of these waiting lists. The wages of workers in that industry rose sharply as their claims were passed on as increased prices. More accurately, we should see *degrees* of elasticity, and *degrees* to which employers are able to pass on increased wage costs to customers. Low-paid workers are often caught by this economic logic: they cannot press wage claims because their employers cannot raise their prices, possibly because they are in a highly competitive industry.

Another important aspect is the perishability or otherwise of the product. If employers can store their product, this will enable them to hold out against a strike whilst still supplying their customers from stocks. Newspapers may not appear to you to be very perishable in the everyday sense of the word, but no-one wants to buy yesterday's news. Workers in the newspaper industry are, therefore, in a very strong bargaining position.

A temporary advantage occurs when there is a sudden increase in demand. With time employers may expand their capacity, but in the short term they will probably ask their employees to work overtime. Employees are placed in a stronger bargaining position for as long as that situation lasts. The opposite is true when there is a sudden decrease in demand. It will take time for employees to find other jobs, and whilst the firm or industry is contracting they are in a weak position.

It is already apparent that the state of the labour market —labour market*s*, more accurately—is highly relevant to bargaining power. Craft unions, as we have seen already, deliberately restrict the supply of their skills to keep up the price of their labour. There is little, however, that unions can do about the demand for the product, and it is this which determines demand for a particular type of labour.

Whatever the conditions of the product and labour markets, a high degree of trade union organisation will strengthen the workers' hand. This is easier to accomplish where workers are employed in large groups. Industries which are characterised by small firms, such as hotels and catering, are difficult to organise. Unfortunately, this is one of those cases where nothing succeeds like success. Where unions cannot show that they have done much for workers they find it difficult to recruit members. Once unions start getting concessions from employers, they find it easier to recruit, and this adds to their bargaining power.

Closed shops

Objections to closed shops are usually based upon ideas of individual liberty. An individual, it is said, should have the right to belong or not to belong to a union. This is an important principle and is enshrined, for example, in German basic law. However, some realities of the situation have to be remembered. Labour is organised into bargaining units to match the power of organised capital. A division in the ranks of labour is not matched by one on the employer's side. We cannot have dual standards. If it is right for the company to bargain as one, there is nothing morally wrong in their employees' doing the same. In practice the bargain which is finally struck applies to all employees, including any non-trade-unionists. Unions resent non-members getting the benefit of their efforts, when in fact they tend to weaken their bargaining power. In this situation there is something in the old maxim that he who is not with us is against us—in strictly bargaining terms.

The basic idea of a closed shop is to ensure that employees get the best possible bargain so far as it is affected by the degree of organisation. Questions of artistic, political or religious freedom are different, although it is possible that in some circumstances these freedoms may be jeopardised. This point is returned to in a later chapter. For the majority of closed shops in manufacturing industry, these questions scarcely arise.

The question of recognition

A union is recognised when it is allowed to negotiate with employers—when it is in fact a recognised bargaining agent. Opposition to a union being recognised may come from employers or other unions. Manual workers have traditionally fought for their unions to be recognised; sometimes literally, more often through strikes. Quite recently there have been some long and bitter strikes on this question. The strike at Fine Tube's went on for three years before the union side admitted defeat (1970–73). Increasingly, the government's conciliation services are being used. Broadly speaking, they proceed on the principle that the majority of workers want to be represented by a trade union, and that the union in question will be able to give them adequate service.

Objections may come from other unions who are already recognised or who think that there is a good chance that they will be. The problem here is to decide which is the appropriate union. The TUC's Bridlington Principles[1]

---

[1] See Chapter 5, page 68.

may be used to decide which union has the right to recruit these workers, and that pre-empts the recognition question. This problem has, however, led to strikes, one of the most notable being in the steel industry over the representation of white-collar workers. The government's services are also used in this connection. Everything written in this and the second chapter on unity of interests has a bearing, so that it is by no means an easy question even for an independent third party.

FURTHER READING

This is given at the end of the next chapter.

QUESTIONS FOR DISCUSSION

1   Are bargaining units designed to give social justice?
2   In what circumstances might closed shops pose a real threat to personal freedom?

10

The Practice of Collective Bargaining

This chapter is concerned mainly with collective bargaining as it takes place between unions and employers or their managers. The role of government and effects upon employers are dealt with elsewhere. Some comments made here might strike the reader as outrageous, but they should be seen in context and judgement reserved until the end of the book.

Collective bargaining has three broad aspects. One is the subject matter of *joint control*, which might also be described as 'possible causes of dispute'. Since wages are usually given top priority in negotiations, some emphasis has been given under this heading to the way that unions justify their claims. Not entirely separate is the question of *procedures* by which disputes can be resolved without resorting to industrial action. Strictly speaking, this is merely another subject for negotiation and a possible cause of disputes. That is a little pedantic, however, and it still seems worth while giving separate attention to procedures. Thirdly, there are the *sanctions* which can be applied if negotiations break down or there is a final failure to agree. Industrial action by employers, such as lock-outs, are no longer a significant feature of the British scene, and there is nothing to be added to what has already been said in connection with employers' organisations. Under this last heading there is an outline of the incidence of strikes in Britain and of observable trends, with some warning about their interpretation.

The subject matter of collective bargaining

There are two sides to any wage bargain. On one side is the amount, quality and type of effort provided by the labour force (including, of course, the conditions in which work is performed). On the other side is the reward for such efforts, including not only wages but 'fringe benefits' such as sickness or pension schemes. Since funds are never unlimited in any employment, union negotiators must decide on which half of the equation they are to operate or what balance to strike between the two. Shorter working hours or better conditions will put up the cost of labour to an employer, and to that extent unions will have to forego some increase in wages if they pursue that line. During the actual negotiations, offers and counter-offers will recognise this essential relationship. Management, for example, may prefer to offer a longer holiday rather than an increase in pay. It follows that even the simplest bargaining is not entirely a question of money. Almost anything that affects employees may be laid on the table.

Payment systems

Payment systems have the vital function that once an agreement has been made they keep employers' job requirements in line with employees' expectations. To the extent that they are successful, they remove any further bargaining opportunities. However, they are not always successful and can be the cause of disputes. Industrial relations is very much concerned with payment problems in that light. The subject is complicated, as one might expect, bearing in mind the complexity of the task which payment systems have to perform. Within the space available, however, we can examine some of the reasons why the *method* of payment is often as important as the amount of pay.

Strictly speaking, a 'payment system' is a particular method of rewarding an employee's work. Work may be paid purely on a time basis, say, so much for a forty-hour week. Provided employees are in attendance for that period, they are entitled to the amount of pay specified. Quite different systems try to encourage greater efforts from employees: this set is referred to rather misleadingly at times, as 'payment by results', usually abbreviated to PBR. We have already touched on this subject in the chapter on management, so that readers should have some idea of the type of systems referred to.

Wages are rarely based entirely on PBR systems. A basic time rate is paid and then a bonus element added. There are many other possible elements, including 'premium payments' for working overtime or in shifts. The 'mix' or proportions of these elements is referred to as the 'pay structure'. A high PBR element in pay packets means that earnings are liable to vary. If they vary too much then workers may not be able to meet their regular commitments. This is bound to have an unsettling effect which will be reflected in the state of labour relations. No definite maximum for the PBR element is fixed, although about one-fifth of the pay packet is commonly used as a rough guide.

Groups of workers have different attitudes to PBR. Oddly enough the attitude varies in different parts of the United Kingdom, PBR being more popular in the north than it is in the south. Some workers detest financial incentive and others see it as giving them a measure of control over their earnings—breaking some of the alienation, one might say.

Workplace relationships are affected by the choice of system. Workshops with an efficient financial incentive scheme tend to be self-regulating. Workers keep at their tasks to earn more money. Time rates throw more responsibility onto supervision. Financial incentives are attractive to management on this account, since they offer to remove a burden from their shoulders. Employees can also prefer a system which keeps supervisors 'off their backs'. Changing from a PBR system to a time rate alters the basic relationship between workers and management, and has on occasion led to strikes. In 1971 women workers in British Leyland went on strike to keep a fairly simple financial incentive scheme in preference to a more sophisticated version.

A system may be entirely inappropriate to a particular job. Just imagine what the results might be if policemen were paid a bonus on the number of arrests they made. Industrial relations can be seriously affected by a system that is inappropriate to any marked degree. Any kind of individual incentive is pointless where teamwork is important. In that case a group bonus is more appropriate, but that may put quite a heavy burden on the shop steward's shoulders as he tries to resolve bickering within the group. Perhaps the group feels that one worker is not pulling his weight. Depending on circumstances a plant-wide or factory-wide scheme may be more appropriate. If work is considered particularly dangerous, unions will fight tooth and nail to prevent financial incentives, because working faster may increase the rate of accidents. The type of work involved has to be considered carefully before any system is adopted.

You will remember that work-studied incentives were designed to overcome the unfairness of relating pay to physical output. An example from the steel industry illustrates the same point on a plant-wide basis. Workers used to be paid a bonus on the tonnage produced by their plant. No doubt for some workers there was a direct connection between their efforts and the output of their plant as compared with another. Maintenance men in an old plant, however, found themselves working harder to keep it going, whilst earning less tonnage bonus than their counterparts who were fortunate enough to be working with the most up-to-date equipment. Shortly after nationalisation, when most of these men were working for the British Steel Corporation, the system was abolished.

A refinement of tonnage bonus takes account of the value of work in money terms. In shipbuilding such a 'weighted' tonnage bonus is used, because a sophisticated vessel requires so much more work per ton than, say, a giant tanker. Value added, however, depends on market prices for the product, and is liable to objections on that account.

A joiner in shipbuilding could find himself earning less than he might in shop-fitting.

Relating earnings to output is at best a somewhat dubious system. In particular, it requires workers to have a great deal of information: they have to be able to monitor production figures, especially on a plant-wide or factory-wide basis, from ready access to the firm's books. This point is better taken up in connection with wage claims based on profits or productivity, and we shall come to it later.

Factory politics, meaning the location of effective power and thus areas of possible confrontation, is affected by payment systems. Under the heading of 'Work study' in Chapter 7 we noted that work-studied incentives can increase the authority of shop stewards by granting more opportunities for bargaining on the shop floor. Time rates, by contrast, tend to increase the authority of full-time officials because they lend themselves to re-negotiation at much longer intervals. Part of the reason for the motor-vehicle industry being so strike-prone lay in the widespread use of direct incentive schemes in a situation where strong shop stewards competed with each other. There has been a general shift towards 'measured day work', which is another type of work-studied incentive scheme. Workers are paid constant earnings in return for an agreement to maintain a certain level of performance, over, say, a month. This is more stable and is less directly related to day-to-day performance. As managements usually have to 'buy themselves out' of an inappropriate scheme, the method as well as the amount becomes fodder for negotiation.

Payment for overtime presents both unions and management with one of their greatest headaches. Unions over the years have fought to reduce the working week, and they are distressed to find their efforts frustrated by members working longer hours for overtime pay. For their part, management are often doubtful about the necessity for overtime. They sometimes think that work could well have been completed within the normal working day, that they ought not to be asked for overtime payments. An important distinction here is between occasional overtime, that which is justified by exceptional circumstances, and systematic overtime—overtime which is worked every week. It is systematic overtime that is the problem, and it is not exclusive to areas of low pay.

Pay rates

Claims about the level or amount of pay are the commonest approach adopted to collective bargaining as we now know it. Claims can be justified under a number of headings:

- (a)   Comparability
- (b)   Cost of living
- (c)   Profits
- (d)   Productivity

(a) *Comparability*   A claim may be advanced on the argument that other employers give better wages and/or conditions. This argument is improved if a comparison can be made in the same locality, although this is not essential. Comparisons can also be made with different grades of work within the same firm. Skilled workers or supervisors may protest that their differential over the pay of lower grades has been reduced. Their claim is usually to restore their differential in percentage terms. Rather similar to the question of differentials is that of *relativities*. A whole bargaining group, composed of many grades, may claim that their earnings are not as high as they should be when compared to some other group or groups. Coal miners often compare earnings in their industry with those of others, believing that they should be 'top of the league'.

This approach is essential to those who are outside the free play of the labour market. Policemen, for example, are not free to take strike action. In settling their pay and conditions some comparisons have to be made with the private sector.

(b) *Cost of living*   Price increases mean that a worker's pay does not retain its purchasing power. Claims are advanced to restore 'real wages', that is, the same purchasing power. Ever since the last war, price increases have called for the upward adjustment of wage rates. Between the wars prices fell and wages were reduced. However, in general wages are 'sticky' downwards, because they are more easily adjusted upwards than downwards.

(c) *Profits* Employees of a firm making large profits will assert that they are entitled to a larger share of this increased revenue, seeing themselves as the people who produced the extra wealth. On rather more rare occasions employees may accept reduced wages or forego an increase to save a firm in financial difficulties. This happened in 1974 with employees of Aston Martin Lagonda, a small-scale manufacturer of exclusive motor cars.

The financial success of an employer is a factor in all negotiations where there is a product market. The last chapter described how this affected a union's bargaining power. At any set of negotiations there will be some idea as to the funds which are available and this must govern the target of negotiators on both sides. That is the fact of the matter.

Within a particular area of employment the *logic* of this argument is at least dubious. When shareholders as a whole are better off, then labour as a whole may fairly claim a share of the community's increased wealth. But it is hard to see why a management should have to pay more for its labour simply because it is more efficient than others. After all, it is not expected that they will pay more for their electricity or raw materials. Profits vary with many factors outside the efforts of a firm's labour force, and when profits are very low, trade unions may be the first to deny any connection. Logically, unions cannot have it both ways, claiming that increased profits result from their members' efforts but that reduced profits are none of their doing.

The argument of profitability, it must be noted, cuts across the principle of comparability. There seems to be no good reason why one worker putting in just as much skill and effort as another should be paid any more or less. But this is likely to happen when profits are taken into consideration, simply because they depend on so many factors outside a worker's control.

The current demand for more information to be given to trade unionists has a bearing on profits, although it applies equally well to productivity. Under the Employment Protection Act, 1975, employers now have a duty to provide unions with information necessary to collective bargaining or 'in accordance with good industrial relations practice'. We are waiting for a 'code of practice' to be published which will state what information is in accordance with good industrial relations.

Trade unions find one practical difficulty at present when trying to base a claim on profits. A company's accounts are primarily directed at their shareholders, to show why a certain dividend is justified. They need not be broken down to give information on individual plants. Faced with global company figures, union representatives for a plant have no idea as to what profits that particular plant did or did not make. The assumption made is that, with more detailed figures, unions will be able to bargain more effectively.

Leaving to one side the question of whether profits are at all relevant, there are some further practical difficulties for trade unions to face. Accountancy is a skilled profession. With pardonable exaggeration in this context, one might say that it takes one accountant to understand another. Given good faith between the two sides, useful and readily-understood information will be provided. But if relations are already bad, a shop steward or even a full-time official in this setting would be a mere amateur confronting a professional. Trade unions will surely need the services of their own accountants in negotiations.

There are, I believe, much sounder reasons for disclosure of information than the discovery of 'hidden profits'. It is highly relevant to the whole business of joint control, and this argument will recur in later sections.

(*d*) *Productivity*   'Productivity bargaining' is a technical term applied to agreements which aim to secure increased productivity *in the future*. This is the peculiar feature of this type of bargaining. All the others have to do with events which have already taken place. Productivity bargains are in many ways declarations of intent. Both sides promise to do certain things which, it is hoped, will lead to greater productivity, and thus to more revenue, higher profits and better wages. When governments control this type of bargaining they usually insist that there should also be some benefit to customers: a three-way split, you might say.

A practical difficulty which you may have noticed already is that at the time the agreement is signed nothing has actually happened. There are no real savings to distribute. But trade unions are almost obliged to ask for 'cash in advance.'.

The crux of the matter is that unions receive extra wages in return for surrendering some small part of their workshop control. The idea is that management are then able to deploy their workforce better and so reduce labour costs for a given output. Plumbers, for example, may agree that electricians can fix their own conduit (piping to carry cable) instead of having to wait for a plumber to do it. Another category concerns the tools of the trade. General workers may on occasion be allowed to use a craftsman's tool to effect some minor adjustment necessary to keep production going. A third category has to do with manning levels; craftsmen may agree to work without mates.

These changes in working practice mean that the unilateral control of trade unions is to an extent surrendered to the joint control of management and unions. Instead of being determined solely by the union, working practice is now the subject of negotiation. There is therefore a fundamental change in factory politics. For this reason the 'hard-liners' amongst craftsmen remain bitterly opposed to productivity bargaining. It also follows that productivity bargaining is more likely to be successful in detail in a particular plant than on a national scale, where it might challenge a craft union's whole philosophy.

Because productivity bargains mark a fundamental change of attitude on the part of some unions, the opportunity is frequently taken for a fairly comprehensive review of a firm's industrial relations and management techniques. New committees are usually set up to monitor progress in new areas of joint control. Modern management techniques themselves often call for more joint control. A job evaluation scheme will usually provide for some sort of appeals committee manned by both sides. In this way management surrender part of their prerogative as well as unions.

This type of bargaining has been encouraged by incomes policies which would only allow wage increases above a fixed limit in special circumstances, including an increase in productivity. It was very fashionable in the late sixties under the incomes policy of that time, when some agreements were undoubtedly designed with the purpose of getting round that regulation. Others were more genuine.

As an answer to bogus agreements, governments have asked for some proof of increased productivity. The Conservative's 'Stage Three' Policy in 1973/4 made it a condition of any settlement above the norm. This stipulation, however, goes against the grain so far as trade unions are concerned. They see wage increases as the price of their co-operation with new working arrangements. They are not usually prepared to surrender part of their unilateral control on the chance that there will be some unspecified gain in the future.

Trade unions are justified in many circumstances in having great reservations. They require a lot of information from the firm on all costs before they can measure the precise extent of their contribution, so the question of disclosure of information is vital. If the new arrangement has saved floor-space, how much has it saved and what is its rental value? Estimating the actual savings can be extremely difficult, even for a firm with tight cost controls.

High unemployment rates in recent years have caused unions to view productivity bargains with some apprehension. In manufacturing industry there has been a fall in employment from 9·2 million in 1961 to 7·4 million in 1975. Faced with that sort of trend, unions are not inclined to create further vacancies by increasing output per man. In so far as restrictive practices may contribute to an industry's decline, that attitude may not be entirely logical, but it is understandable as the immediate reaction of workers facing imminent unemployment. It is noticeable that workers whose occupations are not threatened, electricians for example, are more prepared to negotiate a productivity agreement than, say, shipwrights. Expanding industries find it easier to bargain in this way.

Technological changes must force some bargaining along these lines, because they change job requirements. The same working practices are not appropriate. A change of name might well be beneficial here, but this takes us to the next question about the whole range and purpose of bargaining of any sort.

Range and purpose of collective bargaining

'Bargaining' is a deceptive term on two counts. It implies, at least to the uninitiated, that it is entirely about money matters, and that is not true. Whenever management meet unions on any topic subject to joint control, this is referred to as collective bargaining. But money may not even be mentioned. Changes may be made to working methods to ensure safer working without any extra cost being involved. Even if there is extra cost, unions may not be prepared to discuss it on principle.

More damaging to the purpose of joint control could be the assumption that one side may only gain at the expense of the other. This is true of most wage claims, though not all. Negotiations can lead to a net gain, as with productivity bargains. There are other subjects where it is in the interests of both sides to co-operate: training programmes are one example, since obviously employers need a supply of suitably qualified people. Trade union co-operation is essential if they have fixed quotas on the number of apprentices. Some unions have a more positive interest. NALGO was a professional institute before it became a trade union, and it continues with this activity. Some union journals have technical pages to keep their members abreast of latest developments. Joint control occurs with the Joint Industry Board for Electrical Contracting, which sets the standards for various grades of electrician.

Training is only one aspect of manpower planning and this is a possible area of joint control that cries out for expansion. From their registers craft unions know the available manpower in specific skills. But this has to be matched to employers' requirements at present and in the future. Without co-operation each side is capable, perhaps unknowingly, of frustrating the other's policies. A union seeing a scarcity of jobs might adopt restrictive practices, perhaps tighten up apprentice quotas, when employers in a year or two are desperate for that skill. Bottlenecks of this type are generally agreed to be too common in industry. They might be avoided with more joint control.

A criticism of the shipbuilding industry made by the Commission on Industrial Relations was that there was too little joint control; too much fell under the unilateral control of unions or management.[1] The record of that industry lends some point to their criticism.

This is not entirely an economic consideration. Collective bargaining is the chosen path of British trade unions to increase industrial democracy. The list of topics which might be included is virtually endless. One obstacle is that unions are not always prepared to see the extension of joint control as a two-way process. Industrial democracy has a chapter to itself where collective bargaining is compared to other possible methods of promoting participation (Chapter 12).

---

[1] CIR Report No. 22, Shipbuilding and Shiprepairing (HMSO 1971).

Procedure

Any alteration to those items which are already subject to joint control, by definition has to be agreed by both sides. Anybody contemplating a change needs to know if it falls into this area, and the correct procedure for obtaining authorisation. This is one function of procedural provisions. Allied to it are agreed methods for changing the rules. As the Code of Practice[1] on industrial relations puts it:

'Procedural provisions should lay down the constitution of any joint negotiating body or specify the parties to the procedure. They should also cover:

(i) the matters to be bargained about and the levels at which bargaining should take place;

(ii) arrangements for negotiating terms and conditions of employment and the circumstances in which either party can give notice of their wish to re-negotiate them;

(iii) facilities for trade union activities in the establishment and the appointment, status and functions of shop stewards;

(iv) procedures for settling disputes and individual grievances and for dealing with disciplinary matters;

(v) the constitution and scope of consultative committees.'

Trade unions are keen to see 'status quo' clauses included, and these are now fairly common. They are intended to prevent *any* alteration being made whilst it is still in dispute. Management may think that a particular decision is within their prerogative and, therefore, does not need to be negotiated. Their employees may think differently. The following example is taken from the TUC's

---

[1] Prepared by the Department of Employment to give practical guidance for promoting good industrial relations (HMSO, 1972).

'Good Industrial Relations: A Guide for Negotiations':

> 'It is agreed that in the event of any difference arising
> which cannot be immediately disposed of, then what-
> ever practice or agreement existed prior to the dif-
> ference shall continue to operate pending a settle-
> ment or until the agreed procedure has been ex-
> hausted.'

Another primary aim of procedural agreement is to
provide for the peaceful settlement of disputes *as near as
possible to the point of origin*. Previous comments on productivity bargaining illustrate a general rule that there is more
room to negotiate at lower levels. Relations between shop
stewards and supervisors are of critical importance in this
respect. Workers with a grievance are usually expected to
take it up with their immediate supervisor in the first
instance. Some agreements allow the shop steward in at
this stage if the individual so wishes, but a meeting between
the shop steward and supervisor concerned ought at least
to be the second stage on individual grievances. Collective
disputes, perhaps on wages, are nearly always outside the
jurisdiction of a supervisor and they begin at a higher level,
but the same principle applies.

Failing agreement in the first stage, there is (or ought to
be) *a right of appeal*. Natural justice demands this, and there is
the practical consideration that higher levels of authority
have the chance to intervene before any industrial action is
taken. The final stage in negotiations may, perhaps, be a
meeting between full-time national officials of the union or
unions involved and representatives of the employers'
national organisation; it all depends on the structure of the
bargaining unit.

Provision can be made for arbitration. Both sides have
to agree to take a particular case to arbitration, although
the body to arbitrate may be specified.

Impatience at the time taken to go through procedure
can cause unconstitutional strikes which defeat the whole

object of formal agreements. It is recommended that a time limit is set on each stage.

Agreements of this type have what might be described as an educational function. Shop stewards and management learn about the nature and extent of their responsibilities, which can itself lead to an improvement in industrial relations. All employees ought to know something of the collective bargaining machinery that exists. Even where there are no unions, it is now a legal requirement that employees should be advised of the procedure for handling individual grievances and matters of discipline.

Herein lies one reason for not having legally enforceable agreements. To fulfil its educational role, written procedure has to be in a language that all can understand, and this is not true of contracts which are designed to be legally enforceable. Good legal practice in this respect makes for bad industrial relations. Contract law has always held, despite common belief, that not all agreements are suitable for litigation.

Trade union sanctions

So much for the force of argument. We turn now to the question of sanctions which unions may apply.

Strikes

It is open to the seller of any commodity to hold out for a fair price. Negotiations take place within margins. From the outset unions have an idea as to the least they will accept and management have decided the most that they will concede. On wage negotiations the union side have it in mind that unless they reach a certain figure they will at least threaten to withdraw their labour. Management for their part have fixed a figure above which they are prepared to take the strike. There is a good deal of gamesmanship about all this, as each side tries to guess the other's hand. Although management and unions try to avoid strikes, there could hardly be a process of bargaining without a possibility that the supplier (the union) would refuse to sell below a certain figure, or that the employers would refuse to pay more than a certain amount.

Overtime bans

Union members refuse to work more than their minimum number of hours. In service industries where overtime is essential upon occasion, unions may find this as effective and less painful from their point of view than calling a strike.

Work to rule

Members observe working rules to the letter. When this was done on the railways it was discovered that it prevented trains from running. Employers who are vulnerable to this form of action dread it more than a strike because they still have their workers on the pay roll.

Withdrawal of co-operation

It is rather hard to define exactly how this differs from working to rule. The phrase is often used where there is no precise written set of working rules and it means that employees are as awkward as they can be without actually breaking their contract of employment

Sit-ins, etc.

Workers occupy a premises, usually to prevent a plant from being closed down. A variation of this is a work-in where employees carry on with their jobs as best they can. It is really a denial of management's right to dismiss a group of workers. More comical variations have been used, such as 'whistle-ins', where workers sit whistling a tune.

Blacking

Workers refuse to touch certain work. Dockers, for example, may refuse to load a particular cargo. This tactic is most commonly used where one group wishes to demonstrate its sympathy with another which is already on strike. When employers try to contract work out they may find that other union firms have 'blacked' it.

Picketing

When a strike is in progress union members stand outside the firm to draw their grievance to the attention of other workers and the general public. Members of trade unions such as delivery men are not expected to cross picket lines. Picketing may be used to publicise a dispute even where there is no strike in progress.

There is some difficulty in defining just how far pickets should go in attempting to prevent traffic in and out of a firm. The law is rather vague but obviously seeks to prevent violence. Police on the spot are left with the onerous task of deciding when pickets have exhausted their rights to picket peacefully and are now creating an obstruction.

Incidence of strikes and their interpretation

It has long been a common belief that there was a connection between the size of plants and the incidence of strikes. The DoE Gazette for February 1976 contains the results of a long enquiry which provides statistical evidence to support that view. The actual number of strikes in large plants was not greater, but there were more days lost (see Table 3).

That is not necessarily a convincing argument against large plants. A firm may do some cool calculations. The table shows that the incidence of stoppages in plants with more than 1000 employees is just over 2000 days per 1000 employees. An average of two days per worker per year is rather less than a 1% loss of production time. Economies of scale might easily compensate for such a loss.

Bearing in mind that strikes or union sanctions are an integral part of collective bargaining, they can easily be misinterpreted. It should not be thought that a firm or industry with a high incidence of stoppages necessarily has worse labour relations than one with a 'good' strike record. Factors interact to give a rather perverse result. A firm with good enough labour relations to show high profits presents the trade unions with an argument for a wage increase. Of course, there may be a settlement without any industrial action. But within the bargaining process, there is bound to be the occasion when management decides to call the union's bluff—'to take the strike' rather than concede any further. A strike may ensue.

Table 3

Incidence of stoppages by size of plant: annual average for 1971–1973, manufacturing industry (GB)

Plant size (Number of employees)	Number of stoppages per 100 000 employees	Number of working days lost per 100 000 employees
11–24	8·0	14·8
25–99	19·2	72·4
100–199	23·0	155·0
200–499	25·4	329·1
500–999	29·7	719·4
1000 or more	28·7	2046·1

(*Taken from the Department of Employment Gazette, February 1976*)

We cannot ignore the fact that low productivity, absenteeism, and other measures of performance are equally symptomatic of poor labour relations, and yet much less easily resolved. A point made previously bears repetition: unions do not normally cause disputes, they bring them to a focus. You will hear management say that a strike now and then is not a bad thing, that it 'clears the air' rather like a thunderstorm. After a strike labour relations may be much better.

From a trade union point of view, strikes cannot be entirely bad. Efficient unions are expected to be hard bargainers, and they can hardly gain that reputation if they never take action when management call their bluff.

The number of unconstitutional strikes is a different matter. By definition these are in breach of agreement and prove that procedures are not working properly. When the government in the sixties began to be seriously concerned about the state of British industrial relations it was in the context of about 95% of strikes being unconstitutional.

Table 4

Official strikes as percentage of total in the United Kingdom, 1961–1975

Year	Total	Percentage known to be official
1961	2686	2·2
1962	2449	3·2
1963	2068	2·4
1964	2524	2·8
1965	2354	4·1
1966	1937	3·1
1967	2116	5·1
1968	2378	3·8
1969	3116	3·1
1970	3906	4·1
1971	2228	7·2
1972	2497	6·4
1973	2873	4·6
1974	2922	4·3
1975	2282	6·1

Source: Department of Employment Gazette, July 1976
(This information is given in more detail in every issue)

Neither may unofficial strikes be viewed with equanimity. By definition these are strikes called by other authorities than those specified in union rules. They may still be constitutional, in the case of agreements recognising the obsolete nature of union rule books; but something is still basically wrong. The answer lies in the informal system of industrial relations, which gives a *de facto* power to the shop steward movement which is not recognised in union rules. From the point of view of firms, unofficial strikes which are not in breach of agreement may present no serious problem. On the trade union side they are more serious since they show that their structure needs to be revised. Table 4 shows the high proportion of strikes which are unofficial in the United Kingdom.

FURTHER READING

Industrial Relations Code of Practice (HMSO, 1972)
Good Industrial Relations: A Guide for Negotiators (TUC, 1971)
Overtime and Shift Working: A guide for Negotiators (TUC, 1973)
Management and Technology by Joan Woodward (in *Industrial Man*, edited by J. Burns) (Penguin, 1969)
For those with a particular interest in payment systems, *On the Shop Floor* by Tom Lupton (Pergamon, 1963) is perhaps the best introduction
See also relevant sections in 'Donovan', *Trade Unions* (ed. McCarthy) and Clegg's *System of Industrial Relations*, both of which have been previously mentioned.

QUESTIONS FOR DISCUSSION

1   Ought a firm's profits to form the basis of a wage claim?
2   Would a national job evaluation scheme remove the need for collective bargaining?
3   What harm would the legal proscription of strikes do to industrial relations and the national economy?

11

The Role of Government

In theory the British government is a third party to industrial relations and only intervenes in special circumstances. The two principal parties are the employers and employees, who are supposed to settle their own differences. Each side may of course have an organisation to represent its interests. So far as trade unions are concerned 'free collective bargaining' (meaning 'free from government intervention') is the name of the game. In the rest of Europe, the situation is somewhat different because democratic governments were established *before* powerful trade unions. In Britain, home of the industrial revolution, effective unions came before political democracy. The 'third party' theory was born, therefore, under conditions in which unions had no reason to trust governments, since governments deliberately excluded the working class from political life. Governments for their part had no mind to interfere in commercial matters more than absolutely necessary.

Over the years numerous inroads have been made into this theory so that it can now be quite misleading. There is indeed a mass of legislation applying to industrial relations. This is not a book on law and here one can only indicate the areas in which governments have intervened, and their reasons for doing so. It will be seen that almost every Act of Parliament was an exception to prove the general rule: some special circumstances warranted government intervention into matters that otherwise would have been best left to free collective bargaining.

This chapter starts with a section on the *laissez-faire* theory of industrial relations and then discusses the scope of government intervention, both with regard to trade unions and with regard to workers generally and such matters as Health and Safety Law and the Contract of Employment. The decline of *laissez-faire*, with the government as a major employer and government control of the economy, is then considered.

After this necessarily rather long account, there is a summary at the end of this chapter with a note of correction lest readers are left with the impression that free collective bargaining is a complete illusion.

The laissez-faire theory of industrial relations

It has often been necessary to mention the impact which the industrial revolution had upon society's ideas of what was right and wrong or lawful and unlawful. Without wishing to be tiresomely repetitive this theme must be taken up again. In medieval times society believed in such things as a just price and a just wage. Since these were matters of justice, no one found it strange that the state should intervene to fix prices and wages. With the rise of capitalism these ideas were gradually abandoned and men bowed instead to the laws of supply and demand. State regulation was incompatible with rapid developments in industry and commerce under the stimulus of world-wide markets. The arguments of a new class of capitalists were refined by a succession of political-economists, including Adam Smith who wrote the very influential book *The Wealth of Nations*, published in 1776. He taught that it was not the laws of government which brought prosperity to a nation but the competition of individuals, each acting in his own interest. There were universal economic principles which provided the effective regulation, and it was as useless for governments to attempt to interfere with these as to direct the stars in their courses. Economic theory went hand-in-hand with demands for greater political freedom to give rise to the theory of *laissez-faire*: the government ought to abstain from interference in all commercial matters. This ideology did not prevent the state from enforcing contracts of employment. Under the Master and Servant Act of 1823, workers who broke their contract could be arrested and sent to prison.

Before governments were subject to much pressure from trade unions, they found themselves compelled to deal with the worst effects of the industrial revolution. They did not abandon their general belief in *laissez-faire* but provided specific remedies for what they regarded as special or exceptional circumstances. Various Royal Commissions, of which the most famous were the Children's Employment Commissions of 1842–3 and 1862–7, found that women and children in mines and factories were being greatly exploited. Parliament passed Acts which gave a measure of protection to these particular groups, but it never occurred to them to lay down maximum hours of work for every employee. This style of providing specific remedies for special groups of workers rather than establishing a universal code of labour law has persisted to the present day. The ideological basis has shifted from a belief in unrestricted trade to a belief in free collective bargaining. As we shall see, it is only in recent years that Governments have begun to regulate terms and conditions of employment in a comprehensive fashion, rather than leaving such matters to negotiation between employers and unions.

When in the 1870s the state came to accept collective bargaining, it did so very much in the same spirit. Trade unions were to be treated as exceptions to the general body of common law. As will be explained later, they were thus enabled to do things which for anyone else would be unlawful. But once collective bargaining was established it was to be free from government interference. It in effect provided further support for policies of non-intervention, since it could be left to take care of a wide variety of questions. Only if it could be demonstrated that for some reason collective bargaining could not be effective, could the government then intervene.

We still have a general belief in free collective bargaining and anything that the state does is seen as 'intervention'. The very word intervention implies that there is a self-regulating system. When any system is in need of constant attention, perhaps even the hot-water system in your house, then there is room to doubt whether it is in fact self-regulating. That, putting it rather crudely, is the present position with the British system of industrial relations. Our theory scarcely matches the facts as the following paragraphs should make clear.

The scope of government intervention

Since governments are not only concerned with the welfare of trade union members, it is useful to divide their actions into those which have to do with trade unions particularly and those which apply to all employees.

Government intervention with regard to trade unions

(*i*) *Trade union law* At the beginning of the nine-teenth century trade unions were completely unlawful. Memories of the French Revolution haunted the ruling classes of Europe and they were fearful of any combination amongst the lower orders. With the repeal of the Combination Acts in 1824 it was no longer illegal merely to join a trade union. The whole body of law, however, was not rewritten; unions found it a practical impossibility to operate effectively if employers chose to confront them in the law courts. Apart from statutory law, that is, laws made by Acts of Parliament, there is common law, which is sometimes called 'judge-made law' and has been built up over the centuries by decisions which judges have given in particular cases. Common law had come to reflect a liberal outlook and in particular to regard as wrong any action 'in restraint of trade'.

Another necessary condition of a free economy is that contracts should be honoured, and not interfered with by third parties. Trade unions could not help but come into conflict with both of these legal barriers. By not allowing their members to compete for jobs by offering to work for lower wages, they were acting in 'restraint of trade'. Whenever they called for industrial action they were interfering with contracts of employment, which strictly speaking only concerned masters and their servants. By merely contemplating such matters unions were unlawful conspiracies in the eyes of common law.

The case of Hornby *v* Close in 1866–7 demonstrated that unions could not even protect their own funds. Hornby, president of the Bradford branch of the Boilermakers Society sued Close for the return of some branch funds. Bradford justices refused to hear the case because some of the union's objectives were in restraint of trade. The court of the Queen's Bench subsequently upheld their ruling. Unions were proscribed, that is, put outside the protection of the law because they were regarded as unlawful conspiracies.

After the Second Reform Act of 1867, craftsmen who formed the bulk of trade unionists at the time, were given the vote. Being of political importance to both major parties, they were now able to mount pressure for those legal reforms which would allow their unions to operate effectively. The Trade Union Act of 1871 laid the foundation of trade union law by granting the unions special 'immunities'. Common law precepts were left as they were. It was wrong, and still is, for anyone but a recognised trade union to act in restraint of trade or to interfere with a contract of employment.

Treating trade unions as exceptions has led to endless legal difficulties. In any particular case the court must be satisfied that they are dealing with a trade union which is involved in an industrial dispute as defined by the relevant Acts, or Acts, or Parliament. If there is any doubt about the union's status or whether there is a proper industrial dispute, there is no immunity from the law. There is a chink in the union's armour through which the precepts of common law may penetrate. What happens is that when Parliament and the unions think the question has been finally settled, along comes another case with another verdict which throws the whole issue back into doubt.

The role of government is clear enough. They must repeatedly pass acts to vouchsafe to unions rights which they thought they already had. At present it is the Trade Union and Labour Relations Act of 1974 which defines an industrial dispute and seeks to protect unions from common law liabilities. To a certain extent, therefore, the government is responsible for the legal status of trade union activities, which is the same as saying that they are responsible for the existence of unions within a given legal framework.

(*ii*) *Law on disputes*   Two situations call for particular mention. One is where the services of the employees concerned are vital to the overriding interest of the nation, so that an interruption in supply is not tolerated. Workers in the gas, water and electricity industries used to come into this category under the Conspiracy and Protection of Property Act of 1875 as amended in 1919. If their action threatened public supplies it was a crime, a wrong committed against the state, and they were liable to be convicted. That provision has now been abolished, although there are other groups who may not take industrial action, such as policemen and members of the armed forces. The Post Office Act of 1953 makes it a criminal offence for post office workers wilfully to endanger or retard the delivery of mail. No exception was made for the case of industrial disputes. There were no prosecutions following a major postal strike in 1971, but it seems highly unlikely that those taking part were not guilty of a technical crime.

The second situation may be vaguely described as one of national emergency. The Emergency Powers Act of 1920 gives the government special powers after there has been a Royal Proclamation of an 'emergency'. Where industrial action has been taken or is threatened and this, by interfering with supplies, seems likely to 'deprive the community or any substantial portion of the community of the essentials of life', the government has powers to avoid this result.

Their powers are limited and they may still not make it an offence under this act to take part in a strike or to persuade others to take part. Upon a number of occasions regulations have been made, and in the dock strike of 1949 and the gas strike of 1950 troops were used to maintain supplies.

Neither of these situations brings the motives of the workers concerned into doubt. Instead it is asserted that the services of certain workers are essential to the national well-being and that industrial action cannot be allowed to disrupt those services. The problem for our general theory of free collective bargaining is that in a modern, highly-integrated society the services of so many workers are essential to national well-being. When these laws were framed they were intended to deal with exceptional circumstances, and the government cannot declare too many states of emergency whilst pretending to uphold a system of free collective bargaining. The role of government under this heading can be summed up as fixing limits on the scope for industrial action.

(*iii*) *Encouragement of free collective bargaining*　However inconsistent it may appear, the state does play a considerable role *within* the area of free collective bargaining. It remains free in the sense that the government does not stop disputes or impose settlements. There are, however, steps it can take to improve the quality of collective bargaining, without becoming involved in any confrontation with either side of the dispute.

Advice can be given to both sides. We have already seen how the government was drawn into industrial relations in a much more positive way during the First World War. A committee set up in 1917 under the Speaker of the House of Commons, and called the Whitley Committee after him, issued a series of reports. Right up until the Donovan Report in 1968, 'Whitleyism' was the government's blueprint for a model industrial relations set-up. Joint Industrial Councils at industry level were to be established to represent unions and employers' associations, and these councils would draw up both the substantive and procedural agreements for their industries. Within plants there would be consultation rather than negotiation between managers and shop stewards: management would keep the right to make final decisions. Strikes and lock-outs were not to occur until procedure had been exhausted. Considerable emphasis was put on the contribution which workers had to make to the efficient running of their industries. By 1921, 73 councils had been set up and although many of them lapsed in the inter-war years, there was a revival during the Second World War. As might be expected, Whitleyism was the style of industrial relations adopted in any employment connected directly or indirectly with government, and still is for that matter.

After the Second World War, conditions favoured plant rather than industry-wide bargaining, and formal systems were seen to be breaking down, at least in the private sector. A Royal Commission under Lord Donovan issued a report in 1968 which, recognising the realities of the situation, came down heavily in favour of plant bargaining. The main objective was to regularise the position of shop stewards who had, *de facto*, established their power but who were difficult to control because of their highly informal status. Many critics feel that the Commission focused too much on the private sector and in particular on the motor-car industry, to the neglect of other areas where Whitley-type machinery appeared to be working reasonably well. Despite such criticism the report has continued to have a good deal of influence.

The Commission on Industrial Relations was established as a permanent body in March 1969 as a result of one of Donovan's recommendations. This independent body had power to enquire into all manner of industrial relations problems and then to give advice to the parties concerned. In the event the Commission decided to publish its reports, though they were not bound to do so and this may have been a mistake. The CIR has now been scrapped, but the same type of function has been given to the Advisory, Conciliation and Arbitration Service (ACAS) established under the Employment Protection Act of 1975. The Service will be able to publish reports but what may prove more significant is their power to issue codes of practice. One does not break the law by not observing a code, but at the same time the codes may be quoted in evidence, and their authority will carry a lot of weight. A general Code of Practice is already in existence and was originally issued under the old Industrial Relations Act. It has been re-adopted by the present Trade Union and Labour Relations Act, 1974.

'Conciliation' has a special meaning within the context of industrial relations which is crucial to the government's role. It means that the government tries to bring the two sides together to discuss their differences in the hope that this will shorten or avoid any industrial action. Under a system of free collective bargaining, with the few exceptions we have noted, neither side will have broken the law, and the government therefore has no right to intervene to impose a settlement. In any dispute serious enough to attract the government's attention, the government acts as a conciliator. Unfortunately, too many disputes were landing on the Prime Minister's doorstep. The conciliatory function has now been given to ACAS which is not under the control of any Minister, although it acts on behalf of the Crown. This convenient fiction at least keeps disputes at one remove from party politics. Under the Employment Protection Act, 1975, the Service is enjoined to use its best endeavours to solve disputes within the machinery for voluntary collective bargaining.

As its title implies, the Service also has general responsibility for providing arbitration services. It is essential to a free system that arbitration should be voluntary. The government having declared the name of the game to be free collective bargaining cannot with consistency refuse either side the right to hold out for what it considers to be a good bargain. Logically, free collective bargaining is something of a tautology. There could hardly be a process of bargaining if a third party were to constantly intervene.

We would then be back to the notion of a just price or a just wage. But we do not have such notions and the facts of life are that those groups of workers with great industrial power earn much more than those without it. If either side is fairly confident that it will win eventually, it will see no good reason to risk arbitration. Both sides, therefore, must be willing to call a halt, must agree to go to arbitration.

Generally speaking, unions do not take action without a good prospect of winning their claim. The logistics of industrial action, as every union official knows, are that costs are first weighed against possible benefits. When the balance comes out in favour of action, unions take it. There are exceptional cases. Perhaps the union has just miscalculated or there is some fundamental principle at issue (the dismissal of a shop steward would be a good example). But in the normal run of things, a union which has called a strike will not easily be persuaded to arbitration. Similar arguments apply to the employers' side, although they are more susceptible to pressure from the government. There is the further point that most agreements provide a final arbitration stage should both parties wish to take it. In these circumstances it is quite likely that the ACAS will be called in and provide a very useful service. Once a strike is in progress, however, there is even less likelihood that the parties will agree to a course of action which they have already considered and rejected.

The Service may refer cases either to a panel of independent arbitrators or to the Central Arbitration Committee. This committee like, ACAS, acts on behalf of the Crown but is not subject to the direction of any Minister; it has the status of a high court. There is no right of appeal against its decisions unless they err in law or the committee acts outside it authority, in which case common law actions can be brought in the Queen's Bench Division.

Advice, conciliation and voluntary arbitration are the three traditional activities of the state within the area of free collective bargaining. They are easily remembered from the title of ACAS. As we shall see, the state does intervene more than this but these three activities fit the general theory better than others.

Government intervention with regard to workers generally

Much of the legislation which follows was at the instigation of trade unions and may be to their particular benefit but it does apply to workers who are not members of trade unions.

(*i*) *Health and safety law* Despite the fact that in Britain contracts of employment or collective agreements are usually silent on such matters, they must be regarded as part of the total wage bargain. Proof of this is in the existence of 'dirt money' or 'danger money' which unions negotiate upon occasion. In the past there has been a regrettable tendency to 'go for the money' instead of insisting upon better conditions. In other countries, notably the United States, there are negotiated contracts on health and safety. For historical reasons, British unions have tended to leave such matters to the government.

Before national unions were established even for craftsmen and long before the mass of workers were organised, conditions in the mines and mills of Victorian Britain became a national scandal. Anyone who has read Charles Dickens or any other novelist of the period will realise that the Victorians were a sentimental people. It was the plight of a Tiny Tim or an Oliver Twist which disturbed their conscience. Precious little sympathy was forthcoming for any adult male victim of industrial society. Various acts came to reflect that mentality as governments sought to protect women and children.

In keeping with nineteenth-century liberalism, a grown working man was supposed to be able to look after himself. He was a free man, free to make his own contract of employment with a free employer, and it was thought wrong for the government to interfere with all this freedom. Children were different. It was not even plausible to suggest that a seven-year-old child could be held responsible for his contract of employment. It tells us something about the Victorian status of women that they were allowed into the same bracket of people deserving special protection. Here again were exceptions that required a specific remedy.

Through the years governments continued to pass acts which protected certain groups of people in particular premises. Nowhere is a piecemeal approach more evident than in the field of health and safety. Until the latest piece of legislation, about eight million workers were not covered at all. There was a bewildering variety of rules and regulations applying to different places of work, which now has to be brought to some semblance of order. Until that lengthy task is accomplished we have a most striking example of the way that history governs British industrial relations.

Under the Health and Safety at Work, etc. Act of 1974 there has been a major breakthrough. For the first time, all places of work are to be covered. Instead of responsibility being spread over a number of departments, there is now one Health and Safety Commission. It is composed of representatives from both sides of industry and from local government. Working for that Commission there is a single Executive which draws together a variety of inspectorates. The 1974 Act is an enabling one; that is, it gives powers to the Minister to bring in certain orders. In the meantime the old acts remain on the statute books, but one can at least see the beginning of the end of one Victorian legacy.

(*ii*) *Wages Councils and Boards*   Since the Trade Boards Act of 1909 there has been statutory wage regulation covering certain groups of workers. For a number of reasons it may not be possible for workers to develop sufficient bargaining power to obtain a reasonable agreement with their employers. The government provides these workers with what is regarded as a temporary substitute for voluntary collective bargaining machinery. Wages Councils and Wages Boards are composed of representatives of employers and trade unions in an industry, plus independent members. They fix minimum wages for the whole industry, thus making an exception to the general rule that there is no legal minimum wage in Britain. Wages Councils cover over three million workers in a variety of industries. Agricultural workers are covered by two boards, one for Scotland and one for England and Wales. Under the Employment Protection Act (1975), all of these bodies have been empowered to fix any other terms and conditions of employment.

This legislation has a two-fold objective. It aims to give the workers concerned a reasonable minimum wage and to encourage the development of voluntary machinery so that the Wages Council can be abolished. In practice Wages Councils have often acted as barriers to the creation of voluntary machinery. They were seen not as a temporary but as a permanent substitute. Industry-wide bargaining does not stimulate as much trade union interest as does plant bargaining. Employers in plants or shops have not found it difficult to pay wages above the legal minum, and their employees can interpret this as meaning that they do not need a trade union, the union being held responsible for the low national wage which they have agreed to on the Council. The shopworkers' union, USDAW, does adopt a 'two-tier' approach: over and above the terms and conditions fixed by the Wages Council they have domestic agreements wherever they have sufficient bargaining strength. The success of legislation in terms of either wage fixing or trade union organisation is open to doubt. In some industries Wages Councils have been followed by effective voluntary bargaining machinery and wage rates have been considerably improved. What is more difficult to say is that these developments were attributable to the Wages Council rather than other factors which came to bear after the Council was formed.

Perhaps the greatest weakness in the whole argument behind Wage Councils is the assumption that low pay is identified with certain industries. Within most industries, even those which have a reputation for being highly paid, there will be found pockets of low pay, which are not affected by this type of legislation.

(*iii*) *Contract of employment*   Legally the relationship between an employer and employee was indicated by the terms 'master and servant'. Common law tends to perpetuate this attitude and governments have only departed from it very slowly. Although their *laissez-faire* attitude made them unwilling to intervene on behalf of workers, breach of an employment contract by a worker was a criminal offence up until 1875. The Master and Servant Act of 1823 allowed a single justice, who might be an interested employer, to sentence a worker to six months' imprisonment for leaving his job without giving proper notice. Employers on the other hand could dismiss employees without giving any notice. In one year, 1854, over three thousand workers were thus imprisoned. The Master and Servant Act of 1867 gave some improvements. It prevented summary arrest, allowed workmen to give evidence on their own behalf, and said that in future hearings were to be in open court rather than before a single justice sitting in his own home. Breach of contract was still a criminal offence, however, and in 1872 there were over ten thousand convictions. These laws caused considerable trade union agitation and the Employers and Workmen Act of 1875 finally abolished imprisonment for breach of an employment contract. This act provides an example, perhaps, of the debt which all employees owe to trade unions.

Until recently statutory law did not prevent employers from dismissing at will. The Contract of Employment Act of 1963 laid down minimum periods of notice. This act also required employers to give their employees written information about the main terms of their contract. As amended in 1972 the act established the principle of 'Unfair Dismissal'. Employees who were unfairly dismissed were enabled to obtain compensation from an Industrial Tribunal. There have been further amendments and employees must now be given details of most of their

basic terms of employment—or allowed access to them—
as well as being provided with copies of grievance and
dismissal procedures.

(*iv*) *Other statutory terms of employment*   There are many
other acts which regulate the terms upon which people may
be employed. Taken together they represent a considerable
degree of government intervention. The earlier acts were
passed to remedy particular social problems which the
government could not ignore. The latest acts represent the
government's contribution to the 'Social Contract' (see
later section). Nevertheless it is convenient to list them
together. It should already be apparent that governments
have gradually moved into the area traditionally covered
by substantive agreements or individual contracts. The
question arises, does this contradict the principle of free
collective bargaining? That is a question that you may care
to debate, but two points should be borne in mind. Firstly,
nearly all of this legislation applies to all workers and not
just to unionists. Secondly, it is possible through collective
bargaining to improve on the minima which are laid down
by law.

> Truck Acts from 1831 to 1960 have required the
> payment of wages in cash for manual workers. Company
> stores sometimes cheated workers and held them in
> perpetual debt. Such arrangements in any case were
> not in keeping with ideas of free trade.
>
> Children and Young Persons Act, 1933 and 1963,
> together with the Education Act of 1944, control the
> employment of minors.
>
> The Equal Pay Act of 1970 requires that women
> doing the same or broadly similar work as a man be
> given the same pay and conditions.
>
> The Race Relations Act of 1968 outlaws racial
> discrimination in general and in questions of employ-
> ment in particular.
>
> The Disabled Persons (Employment) Act of 1963

requires some firms to employ a proportion of registered disabled.

The Redundancy Payments Act of 1965 provides for payments to employees made redundant.

The Sex Discrimination Act of 1975 seeks to prevent unfair discrimination on grounds of sex.

The Employment Protection Act of 1975. This statute has so many aspects that it defies classification. It formed a large part of the government's answer to the TUC's shopping list under the Social Contract. It deals with two subjects already covered, Wages Councils and Contracts of Employment. Here are some additional items:

Extension of industrial agreements to other employees in the industry;
Guaranteed wages for workers laid off;
Rights for expectant mothers;
Suspension on medical grounds;
Rights on insolvency of employer;
Procedures for handling redundancies and time off for 'job hunting'.

The decline of laissez-faire government

The idea of the government as a third party to industrial relations was more credible under nineteenth-century conditions when the government only had a minor economic function. Today the state is a major employer and has re-assumed overall responsibility for the national economy.

In neither of these roles is it really a third party, because it has a direct and immediate interest in the outcome of negotiations. Both functions have led to increasing intervention in industrial relations, which at times has been to such an extent that it was impossible to pretend that a system of free collective bargaining was in operation. The current Social Contract requires the government to pass certain legislation as the price of trade union co-operation. Such legislation is scarcely likely to be strictly impartial as between trade unions and employers' organisations. Some provisions of the Employment Protection Act have been criticised as being 'collective bargaining fodder', meaning that they give unions benefits that they would normally be expected to obtain through collective bargaining.

(*a*) *The Government as a major employer*   Since the Second World War there has been a tremendous increase in the size of the public sector. Various acts of nationalisation have taken major industries into public ownership, so that we now say that we have 'a mixed economy'. Theoretically, the day-to-day running of these nationalised concerns or 'Public Corporations, to give them their correct title, is the responsibility of an appointed board. It is these boards, rather than the government, who are supposed to bargain with trade unions. In practice, governments openly manipulate the public sector in support of their economic policies. Prices of goods produced by the public sector have been held down below the international market level: coal and steel are the best-known cases. If prices are held down, wages must be under the same constraint because the boards simply cannot afford to give such high pay rises. Quite directly, governments have repeatedly made the public sector bear the brunt of their incomes policies. There is little doubt therefore that the government exerts a considerable influence in the labour market. It is not a third party.

(*b*) *Government control of the economy*   *Laissez-faire* economics died a lingering death. Faced with massive unemployment between the wars, governments still opted out of responsibility but since the Second World War it has been accepted that the government is responsible for the nation's economic well-being. There are a number of objectives: to maintain a high level of employment, to promote economic growth, to control inflation, and to keep a healthy balance of payments.

Unfortunately, these objectives are not always compatible with the same policy. Hoping to cure inflation, the govern-

ment has had to allow unemployment figures to rise. The
major point, however, is that each of these objectives is
affected by the state of industrial relations, and policies in
pursuit of them have important consequences for industrial
relations. In this situation one cannot envisage the government as a distinterested person standing by merely to see
fair play between employers and unions. The whole future
of free collective bargaining is brought into question by this
essential connection between government policies and
industrial relations. If we take each of the major economic
objectives in turn this interdependence can be better
illustrated.

Full or near-full employment is obviously in the interest
of trade unions. A job, after all, is the prime need of their
members. There is also a connection between the level of
employment and the power of trade unions. When the
economy was not regulated, each major slump set trade
unions back on their heels, especially those for general
workers. The power and influence of trade unions today is
largely attributable to post-war, full-employment policies:
there has been no great pool of unemployed to weaken
union bargaining power. In that sense collective bargaining
has not been free from government intervention for many
years, nor is it likely to be in the future.

Economic growth in simple terms means that more is
produced per man. Capital investment is the key to this
problem, since the more power a worker has 'behind his
elbow' the more he is likely to produce. Once productivity
per man is raised then it is possible to raise wages. Capital-
intensive industries tend to pay higher wages. The same is
true when comparing nations; those that are rich in capital
have a higher *per capita* income. One can easily see the
interest that unions have in this topic and they continually
press governments to encourage more capital investment.
To the extent that the state can influence the level of
investment, it is responsible for the level of incomes. There
is very little that trade unions may do for themselves in
this respect.

Inflation, meaning rapidly rising prices, has been a world-wide problem in recent years, from which Britain has suffered particularly. Economists differ amongst themselves as to the root cause of inflation and what should be done about it. The usefulness of incomes policies is in particular dispute. An incomes policy is a polite term for wage restraint. In the midst of mutual recrimination and conflicting advice from experts, each political party has sworn that incomes policies were useless, and promptly adopted one when next in office. Without any doubt they are in flat contradiction of the principle of free collective bargaining. Neither unions nor employers are free to pursue or grant wage levels of their own choosing. As a consequence, instead of keeping out of the ring, governments have found themselves in direct confrontation with unions. When coal miners broke the Conservatives' incomes policy in 1973–74 they virtually forced that party out of office. Thus a government found itself in the very situation that the whole system of free collective bargaining was designed to avoid: a constitutional crisis arising from a confrontation between the state and organised labour.

Britain's chronic balance of payments problem has a bearing on industrial relations. As Britain approaches a high level of economic activity, which means a high level of employment, imports are sucked in at a faster rate than we can increase our exports. The nation tends to go in debt to the rest of the world, and the government is forced to cut back expenditure or reduce economic activity by some method. As a result the unemployment figures go up and trade unions are not at all pleased.

Exports are vulnerable to industrial action. Goods sell not just on price but on delivery dates as well. Naturally, the government is alarmed when a strike holds up exports. It tends to intervene rather quickly and maybe even declare a state of emergency when problems arise. The considerable government interest in the docks has to be understood in this context.

(c)　*The Social Contract*　At present (1976) trade unions are co-operating with the Labour Government in return for legislation which is in their favour. Unions have accepted first wage restraint and then public expenditure cuts mainly to keep the Labour Party in office. From all that has been said about the interdependence of government and trade unions it is obvious that there has to be some sort of understanding between them. The particular feature of the Social Contract is that it is with the Labour Party, not with the government as such. Legislation passed under the Social Contract does not even pretend to be strictly impartial as between unions and employers. Much of the Employment Protection Act, for example, favours trade unions and has not been equally welcomed by employers. Unions are to have information on an employer's business to help them in their negotiations; employers are compelled to give shop stewards time off to attend to union business and go on courses approved by their union or the TUC. Furthermore, benefits granted by this act are only available to 'independent' trade unions. This definition excludes staff associations which are financed and encouraged by employers. This type of intervention goes far beyond the government's traditional role of advice, conciliation and arbitration. It is putting into substantive agreements conditions which unions might have been expected to negotiate for themselves.

Summary and note of correction

After this rather long discussion a summary will be useful. Since we have concentrated on the role of government a note of correction is necessary to restore a more balanced view.

Traditionally we have a system of free collective bargaining, which means 'free from government intervention'. This tradition arose when governments were not supposed to interfere with economic matters. Each act of intervention had to be justified by some special circumstances. Free collective bargaining itself required Acts of Parliament to protect trade unions from common law decisions. Over the years special circumstances warranted a good deal of intervention but the central principle remained intact.

Doubts arise now that the government is itself a major employer and has overall responsibility for the national economy. As governments pursue such policies as full employment, they are responsible for the power and influence of trade unions. Paradoxically, the power of unions may frustrate the government's economic objectives. Some form of understanding has become necessary. Incomes policies, always justified as a temporary expedient, run contrary to the principle of free collective bargaining. Unfortunately, we have had a succession of such policies and it may be doubted whether modern governments can manage without them. Under the Social Contract this present government has dropped all pretence of neutrality. Laws are passed favourable to trade unions in return for their acceptance of wage restraint.

Admittedly, all this adds up to a massive amount of intervention, but any reader who is left wondering whether there is anything remaining of free collective bargaining must bear two points in mind. The first is that despite the government's economic role, we do not have a completely planned economy. Prices are not all fixed by the state; workers can move between jobs, and businessmen plan their own investments to a large extent. In that situation trade unions will always demand the same right as the seller of any other commodity, the right to get the best bargain that they can. There is no easy logical solution to the problems of labour in a free market. Secondly, good industrial relations could never be prescribed by the state or its agents. Independent unions are necessary to represent their members' interests and laws could never hope to cope with all the possible issues. Even where there is a legal regulation, it is only a minimum, which unions seek to improve upon. Human affairs are just as complex and subtle at work as anywhere else. That being the case, there is never likely to be a labour code which would remove the need for the services of good trade union representatives exercising their discretion.

FURTHER READING

Labour and the Law by Otto Kahn Freund (Stevens, 1972)
The Worker and the Law by K. W. Wedderburn (Penguin, 2nd edition, 1971)
Workers' Rights by Paul O'Higgins (best book for shop stewards) (Arrow, 1975)
HMSO publish a series of short guides to Acts of Parliament and the general reader will find these more intelligible than the Acts themselves.

QUESTIONS FOR DISCUSSION

1   Do we still have a system of free collective bargaining in Britain?
2   Is it true that all workers want from the law is for it to leave them alone?
3   Is collective bargaining a liberal or a socialist concept?

12

Industrial Democracy and Participation

The long history of the British labour movement has contained many ventures in industrial democracy. Producer
co-operatives under the influence of Owenite socialism
were seen as an alternative to the capitalist system. Workers'
control of all industry was advocated early in this century
under the joint influence of industrial unionism from the
United States and 'syndicalism' from France. The latter
term might be taken literally to mean simply trade unionism,
but French trade unions had a different historical development from the British. Syndicalism refers to a belief in
industrial action as a means to transform society. Great
faith was placed in the power of a general strike to overthrow the existing system.

However, the form that has taken root is collective
bargaining, which, as mentioned in the first chapter, has
significantly extended the area of joint control. The latest
idea is that of 'participation', meaning in this context the
election of worker's representatives onto boards of directors.
Participation is already highly developed in West Germany and is being promoted by the Common Market Commission.

Such concepts may be seen in a spectrum based on the
degree of workers' control which each implies. At one
extreme is outright worker's control of all industry. A
modified form of this, called 'Guild Socialism', allows con-
sumer's interests to be represented through the state. Producer Co-operatives give workers control of individual firms

but not of whole industries. Participation requires the present owners of industry to share control with workers' representatives. Finally, at the other extreme, there is collective bargaining which allows joint control of those topics which are of immediate interest to labour.

Participation is the subject of much current debate because it is imminent under Britain's membership of the Common Market. There is at present an enquiry being carried out by the Bullock Committee to which all interested parties are submitting evidence. It is, therefore, quite central to this chapter, although the other forms of industrial democracy have to be considered to give some perspective.

Besides setting participation in context, the following notes will introduce the more important ways in which democracy can be measured. We have to have some analytical tools to help us compare one institution with another. Lastly, there are a number of practical difficulties with regard to participation with which you should be familiar. These questions of what might be called the mechanics of participation give rise to some of the most heated controversy.

Producer Co-operatives

Producer co-operatives date from very early in the nineteenth century though their history continues right up to the present day. Groups of workers, with or without the backing of their union, formed self-governing workshops. In Britain they had their greatest impact during the second quarter of the nineteenth century. Trade unions originally welcomed the idea as a means of finding employment for members who were unemployed or on strike. Robert Owen adopted the institution as a means of furthering his socialist aims. Later Christian Socialists fostered self-governing workshops. In 1849 they founded the Society for Promoting Working Men's Associations. In France there were similar workshops associated with another brand of socialism. There is then no particular political philosophy behind the institution and it does not necessarily imply a total rejection of the capitalist system.

Producer co-operatives have a very high mortality rate. By 1854 Christian Socialists had given up the idea completely. The first and final report of their Society stated that each of their workshops had quarrelled with its manager and turned him out within six months. There have been hundreds of other producer co-operatives which have failed within a short time.

Sidney and Beatrice Webb examined the problem and concluded that the institution itself was ill-adapted to survive. There was poor workshop discipline, an inadequate knowledge of the market, and a slow response to technical change. In respect of their last point it is significant that producer co-operatives have been more successful in small-scale industry using little machinery, such as boot and shoe repairing. The Webb's analysis is also relevant to recent attempts at forming producer co-operatives. A Glasgow newspaper had the same difficulty with its management. The motor-cycle works at Meriden miscalculated the American market. Some critics of workers' control base their objections on the premise that management is a highly skilled profession which the average worker cannot be expected to understand. The history of producer co-operatives provides evidence in support of that view. It should not however be taken as conclusive, because a degree of workers' control can be matched with expert management. West Germany's schemes of participation have not had any great difficulties in this respect.

Workers' control of all industry

During the second half of the nineteenth century and up until the period 1910 to 1922, trade unions showed little interest in the direction of industry. In that period interest was renewed under the stimulation of Industrial Unionism from the United States and Syndicalism from France. In this country these two sets of ideas were merged together. There was a common belief that workers should take industrial action to overthrow the state, which was viewed as an instrument of capitalist exploitation. Great faith was placed in the effectiveness of a general strike. There was a strong anarchist element which wanted nothing to do with political parties. Those that were in favour of political activity thought that once workers had control of Parliament they should dissolve it on the spot. The movement offered no positive proposals on the way that society should be organised: all economic questions were supposed to look after themselves once the workers had industrial power, and they were dismissed as 'trivial'.

Guild Socialists were a group of middle-class intellectuals, the most famous being G. D. H. Cole. They had a much more constructive theory to offer. They adopted the idea that industry should be controlled by industrial unions though they wanted to re-name them 'National Guilds'. The reference to a pre-industrial institution was quite deliberate. Their main aim was to restore the workers control over their working lives. But they thought that at the same time they could provide a more efficient system. A series of articles written for a weekly magazine called 'The New Age' in 1912 by S. G. Hobson effectively founded the movement. He attacked the wage system as not only being morally unjust but also inefficient. G. D. H. Cole put the relationship succinctly when he wrote, 'Poverty is the symptom: slavery the disease.'

Guild Socialists also recognised that consumers' interests were not identical with those of producers. Their solution was a division of powers between the State, representing consumers, and National Guilds, representing producers. The State would own all the means of production and industry would be directed by the Guilds. Guilds would have to negotiate with the State over such matters as prices.

At the end of the period in question with the onset of the depression, the British labour movement lost interest in workers' control. A fairly small minority maintains some interest in the subject, and much of what G. D. H. Cole wrote still makes interesting reading.

Joint control via collective bargaining

Collective bargaining is the characteristic method by which modern unions attempt to obtain more control of industry. Despite its undoubted success, it has two weaknesses as compared with participation. It is a 'negative' type of control, in that unions tend to veto management proposals rather than make positive suggestions of their own. It also operates too late in the decision-making process for any fundamental changes to be effected. By the time that unions become involved many options have been closed by previous decisions.

When Abraham Lincoln referred to democracy as 'government *by* the people' he gave the kernel of the idea of 'positive' control. Negative control is quite different and can be summed up as government *with the consent of* the people. People have an active role under the first and a passive one under the second. There is some positive control exercised by unions under collective bargaining. They do on occasion, especially in the context of productivity bargaining, take the initiative on questions of working arrangements or the introduction of modern management techniques. Most bargaining, however, is simply in terms of unions asking for better pay and conditions. There may be some criticism of management if these demands cannot be met, perhaps on the ground of lack of investment. But there is no continuous involvement of trade unions in the formulation of industrial policy.

Basic industrial decisions come before the stage of collective bargaining is reached. The establishment of a completely new factory illustrates the principle: the board of directors will decide what is to be produced and for what market; that decision limits the range of available technologies. Still it is the board which decides to opt for, shall we say, a capital-intensive, continuous-flow method of production. Job requirements are now determined to within very close margins. It is only at this stage that management will be asked to negotiate with unions. These negotiations will match the firm's job requirements with workers' job expectations. But unions cannot claim work which has been planned out of existence; they can only claim those jobs that they recognise. Our consideration in the second chapter of the factors governing the maintenance of craft unionism should come to mind: even where there is a more gradual development which enables unions to hold onto jobs and dictate workshop practice, unions are looking backwards rather than forwards. They cannot be said to be helping to plan technological development. If their industry as a result becomes too backward as compared to overseas competitors, they will put themselves out of work in any case. The decline of British shipbuilding is a possible case.

Wages are also pre-determined to a considerable extent. Here you may recollect some of the determinants of a union's bargaining power. Choice of product and market will affect pricing, the firm's revenue and, therefore, their ability to pay. Different investment decisions give a different pattern of returns over time and this must also affect wage settlements. Whether the industry is capital- or labour-intensive will determine productivity per man, revenue per man and the level of wages. A workforce cannot be paid more than it earns in the long run. In the example given, wage settlements would be fairly high.

Conditions of work, whether a job is boring or satisfying, whether it is clean and healthy or dirty and dangerous, these too will have been already decided to a very large extent. Once a given method of production has been chosen, there is little that unions can achieve through collective bargaining. A conventional, underground coal mine must remain a dirty, noisy, dangerous place to work, even after the union has negotiated pit-head baths and the like. In that particular case an alternative technology may not be available but it clearly illustrates the limits within which traditional collective bargaining operates so far as working conditions are concerned. In other industries such as motor-car manufacture we do have alternatives, and workers on boards of directors would be faced with a choice.

Consultation extends to matters outside the area of negotiation. Trade union leaders are forever asking for 'the fullest possible consultation'. Employers tend to be equally fond of the same cliché. Before pinning too much faith on this process we ought to consider carefully what it means: employers or management who are skilled and experienced in making certain decision and who remain entirely responsible for those decisions ask the opinion of union representatives, whose skill and experience lies in different areas and who will not be held accountable for the decision which is finally made. One must, with the greatest respect, doubt whether such an opinion is worth having. Surely some experience allied to a degree of accountability improves the quality of opinion given on any subject?

Union leaders have been brought up in the collective bargaining tradition. Their members do not expect them to be practised in industrial policy-making. Worker directors would gain some experience and they would be held accountable for their opinions. As a consequence it is reasonable to expect that ordinary union members would raise their expectations. In the field of political democracy Mr Gladstone remarked that it was the right to vote that fitted people to vote. Industrial democracy in areas where workers feel that they and their representatives are in no way responsible is likely to be of a poor quality. Since I could not in all honesty conceal a personal opinion as to the value of consultation, you may note that others set greater store by it.

Some practical considerations

Professional management

Highly technical questions tend to have a correct answer. In advanced areas of technology, scientific principles leave little room for matters of opinion. A Russian-built supersonic airliner turns out to look very like the Anglo-French model. Workers do have an interest in product design, and their jobs depend on the excellence of the product; but that is not to say that as workers they have a distinctive contribution to make. Most people would agree that there is a whole range of questions which are best left to the experts. Normally we expect a fairly high degree of agreement amongst those experts, However much one may equivocate, this type of decision-making does not lend itself to positive-democratic control.

Some critics of participation point to the fact that modern management has become highly technical. A previous chapter on management has already touched upon this subject. So far as participation is concerned, it is alleged that the workers' representatives will have nothing to contribute because they are not experts in management. Straightaway it must be observed that if such critics are to be consistent, then they should object to the presence on boards of those directors who are there simply to watch over their investment. By no stretch of the imagination can one suggest that all of our present directors are highly trained in modern management techniques. Pushing their logic still further a board of directors seems to serve no purpose. There is after all not just one high-level skill involved but whole range of them. Does the finance director understand the technical director? Does the marketing director know what the industrial relations director is talking about? What do these critics suppose a board of directors does?

Presumably there has to be a level of common understanding which allows all these various experts to discuss common problems sensibly. A board of directors is a committee, and it is not the function of committees as commonly understood to provide technically correct solutions to problems. Experts in a discipline confer upon occasion but that is a different matter. A financial director would not start arguing about transistors or piston rings except in so far as they affected his accounting. Worker directors could similarly see the implications of proposals for their members and give an opinion on likely reactions.

There is, furthermore, a fundamental fallacy in the notion that *all* questions are best answered by experts.

Once you have decided that you will build a supersonic airliner, the design of that craft may be very deterministic. But there was room for considerable difference of opinion even amongst the experts as to whether we should have such an aircraft in the first place. I may value the time saved more highly than you do, and I may find the noise level much less disagreeable. Both the benefits and the costs of having such a vehicle involve 'value judgements'. Simple examples of such judgements would be a choice between butter and margarine or red and white wine. All questions are not susceptible to an expert answer.

Value judgements are often concealed in basic assumptions. It may be assumed that workers want higher pay rather than more congenial work. Given that assumption there can be such a tightly-knit logical argument that it will allow of no disagreement. But the assumption need not be right. What the workers want in this respect is the type of question which is susceptible to a democratic answer. As their representatives, worker directors could convey the opinions or value judgements of employees to the board.

Summing up this section, it appears that worker directors need not be highly skilled in modern management techniques. They will, of course, require sufficient knowledge to be able to follow proceedings. They will need to spot implications of policy proposals for their constituents, and this will require some training and practice. They will also need to challenge any unwarranted assumptions. But the logic of the situation does not preclude such representatives from having a positive contribution to make.

Delegate or representative?

Delegates are instructed by their constituents in detail as to what to say and how to vote. Representatives, strictly speaking, are elected to use their judgement on questions as they arise. In common usage we do not make this distinction. Many trade union representatives should be described as delegates. A shop steward, for example, acts as a delegate on all important questions. Members of Parliament, by contrast, are representatives.

The distinction is important in the context of participation because there is a danger of worker directors drifting away from their constituents. In 1964 the Tavistock Institute of Human Relations found this to be the case in Norway. They concluded that the workers' representative 'more and more forgets that he is representing a special interest group.'

As there is a strong tradition of delegation in Britain in the manner of shop stewards, it seems likely that the shop floor will expect to keep worker directors on a fairly tight rein. A TUC delegation to Germany in November of 1968 found many complaints from workers that their representatives failed to report back sufficiently. This is the type of failing that the TUC could have been expected to look for.

We still do not have the government's proposals on participation, but it will be interesting to see what provisions are made for reporting back to the shop floor.

Ownership and control

With the exception of Norway, European forms of participation in the private sector leave the ultimate control of a company with the Annual General Meeting of Shareholders (AGM). The TUC are looking for something like the Norwegian system whereby the AGM will not be able to veto any board decision. For many years the TUC would have nothing to do with participation because they saw the interests of labour and capital as irreconcilable. If the AGM is to be left with the power of veto, then the TUC fear is that worker directors may find themselves working under impossible conditions.

Percentage of worker directors

For the same reasons the TUC is looking for 50% representation on boards by worker directors. This requirement can be more easily met if the board is split into two levels, as it is on the continent. The higher or supervisory level is responsible for policy which is then passed to the lower or managerial level for execution (a point which is relevant to the 'expert management' argument). Worker directors on the continent belong to the supervisory level and the aim of the TUC is that this practice should be adopted in the UK.

Workers' apathy

Less tangible though not less important is the problem of whether workers will in practice show much interest in questions of industrial policy. Previous paragraphs on practical considerations have a direct bearing. Obviously workers are likely to be more interested if they are closely involved with a considerable degree of control. There still seems to be a need for a programme of education.

Yugoslavia's experience of workers' control is of some interest in this connection. Some years ago there was disappointment at the lack of interest shown on the shop floor. Their experience of worker directors was similar to that of Norway with participation. Yugoslavia has moved towards a system based upon delegation at all levels. Workers' councils are something of a left-over from the old system and are being replaced by assemblies (*skupstine*) of delegates for each shop. But a second marked feature of the Yugoslav system is the amount of effort that goes into education in self-management. This starts with induction courses and is a feature of all subsequent training. All economic plans have to be explained to the workers. Schools, universities, newspapers and television are all involved in this effort as well as firms and trade unions. Britain will have to proceed in the light of her own experience, and participation must be regarded as experimental for some years to come but the experience of overseas countries should still help us to avoid unnecessary mistakes.

FURTHER READING

(There is now so much reading on this subject that one hesitates to be selective. Paul Blumberg's book contains a fairly extensive bibliography for those with a particular interest. The DoE Gazette often has relevant articles. In the March 1976 issue there is a most interesting account of 'The self-management system in Yugoslavia'. The Bullock report when it comes out will have to be read.)

Self-Government in Industry by G. D. H. Cole (Hutchinson, 1972)

Industrial Democracy: The Sociology of Participation by Paul Blumberg (Constable, 1968)

See also part two of '*Trade Unions*', edited by W. E. J. McCarthy.

QUESTIONS FOR DISCUSSION

1 On the basis of questionnaires completed by workers, some sociologists conclude that there is no demand and therefore no need for participation. Do you agree?

2 What might employers and unions do to make participation more effective?

3 Should all worker directors be members of a trade union? (Remember the difficulties that unions have had with shop stewards.)

Part Three: Questions of Change

Within the British system of industrial relations, we have already noted much that needs to be reformed. No-one doubts that. Trade unions and employers see the need for unilateral changes and for improvements in their dealings with each other. Putting things in a wider context, it is possible to doubt whether society can afford to leave the problem with trade unions and employers. The basic question is, 'How well do conventional industrial relations fit into modern-day society?' This may usefully be subdivided into four closely-related questions:

1. What is the essential nature of the problem?
2. How serious is the situation?
3. Who is to put things right?
4. What are they to do?

If in answer to the first two you see disorders in the system of free collective bargaining, which only have minor repercussions upon society at large, then you will be inclined to leave it to those concerned to put things right. If there is a serious national economic crisis, the state must be expected to intervene. Obviously, the people or the institutions chosen as instruments of reform will be limited in their powers, and that tends to answer our last question. Recent history has more than adequately demonstrated the limits on what the state can achieve through the force of law.

Chapter 13 takes up the first two questions. On strictly

economic grounds the evidence is not conclusive, but when we take political and social considerations into account, there is an obvious need for some radical re-thinking of our conventional method of free collective bargaining.

Chapter 14 outlines some of the pros and cons of state intervention in general terms, before turning to the practical question of what the state is in fact likely to be able to achieve through legal enactment. Recent history demonstrates that such intervention is likely to be worse than useless where free collective bargaining is concerned. Passing laws which cannot be enforced only brings the law itself into disrepute. Almost inevitably, we are forced to re-examine the essential nature of our problem, and to go back to the alienating nature of industrial work, since this is the root from which our institutions and conventions have sprung.

All parties can make a positive contribution to the reduction of alienation. There is evidence which points trade unions, employers and management in this direction, especially if they are prepared to consider developments in other countries. The government has already set up a unit to examine this aspect of industrial relations.

However, there are limits to what can be done within society's existing set of priorities. Alternative technology with its marked shift away from materialist goals is, therefore, introduced as a final section. This may be rather futuristic, but it opens the mind to some exciting possibilities.

Pressures on the Present System

A great deal of attention has been paid throughout this book to historical factors. This has been necessary in order to understand the present state of British industrial relations and the relations of British trade unions to international and world-wide organisations. That this type of explanation should be so necessary is an indication that the rationality of much that goes on is doubtful. History is not, therefore, a waste of time. Karl Marx observed that we study history in order to get rid of it. In industrial relations this can be taken to mean that once we understand the reasons for our institutions and conventions, we are better able to decide whether in fact they are relevant to our present situation. Reasonable people are always hesitant to interfere with something they do not quite understand. Historical explanation ought to give us the confidence to make necessary alterations. Before proceeding to consider further pressures a brief summary of the major contradictions or anomalies will be useful.

Trade unions were called into being because of the effects upon workers of the industrial revolution. The very nature of industrial work is a crucial concept. The role of modern trade unions has been largely in acceptance of technological decisions, although these decisions are at the root of their grievances. When they have objected to innovations, through craft unionism, their contribution has been rather negative. They have not themselves been associated with positive proposals for alternative arrangements. Even revolutionary trade unionism has largely ignored economic problems, as industrial unionism did, or has harked back to a pre-industrial age as producer co-operatives seem to do. Collective bargaining has made important contributions to industrial democracy through the years by extending the area of joint control. It seems doubtful, however, whether this can provide the radical solutions that seem to be called for. In any case free collective bargaining does not obviously provide social justice as between one group of workers and another. Bargaining power has many factors which are quite outside the control of workers; the elasticity of demand for the product is an example. The whole idea of trade unions providing an adequate countervailing power to that of organised capital is open to doubt in the context of multi-national companies.

Within trade unions there are problems. As the branch has decayed so has the original theory of trade union democracy. The forum for discussions has shifted from the branch to multi-union meetings at the workplace, and yet these remain outside union rule books. Shop stewards and their joint committees have a power which still goes largely unrecognised by formal institutions. Whether or not one agrees with industrial unions, there appears to be some need for unions to be re-structured to meet the requirements of modern industry. That is not the end of the problem, for the representativeness of top officials and even the TUC, particularly in the area of politics, is questionable. The difference between TUC voting figures and a national plebiscite on the Common Market is a case in point. Democracy as government by consent is dubious when there is an overriding economic motive for trade union membership, and members do not therefore show their dissent to political policies.

The role of the state is now so complex as almost to defy description, so far has practice departed from original theory. The state is not in fact a third party to industrial relations; it is an active participant. Incomes polices cut clean across the principle of free collective bargaining. As a result one government was drawn into direct confrontation with the coal miners and lost the consequent general election (1973). Under the terms of the Social Contract to which employers were not a party, the government is not impartial as between the two side of industry.

That summary might be thought to contain enough evidence to convince anyone that there is a serious situation calling for a radical remedy. It does not, because the harm done to the national economy is disputed. Even the case for incomes policies is not proven; some economists and politicians believe that they are irrelevant to the problem of inflation. If incomes policies and other forms of intervention were not necessary, the government can be said to have only themselves to blame for getting their fingers burned in the past or for the present state of affairs. They should, it could be argued, have left well alone. There is no need in this context to distinguish between the two parties which have been in office, because they have both paid heavily on more than one occasion for their interventionist tactics. This is an appropriate point to review the economic significance of strike statistics from a national point of view.

Strikes and the national economy

International comparisons are often made of the number of strikes and the number of lost working days. The International Labour Office collects this data and it is published annually in the Department of Employment Gazette. Table 5 is taken from last December's issue. In certain contexts these statistics no doubt have their value, but they do not show the vulnerability of these nations to strikes. When looking at these tables we should ask ourselves a number of questions. Are these nations, like Britain, heavily dependent on overseas trade? Are their governments borrowing large sums from abroad to finance public expenditure? Do they have chronic balance of payments problems? What are their rates of inflation, of economic growth, of unemployment, and so on? The argument about whether Britain is strike-prone may prove to be irrelevant.

Table 5

International Comparison of
Days Lost per 1000 people employed
(Average for ten years 1965–1974)

Italy	1665
Canada	1644
United States	1305
India	1136
Ireland	1018
Australia	913
Finland	810
United Kingdom	743
Denmark	511
Belgium	334
New Zealand	322
France	274
Japan	243
Netherlands	65
Norway	60
West Germany	50
Sweden	46
Switzerland	1

(*Source: D of E Gazette, December 1975*)

These tables do not indicate specific economic damage. Strikes in export industries are bound to damage relations with overseas customers if goods are not delivered on time. Strikes in the docks will hold up supplies of imports which are essential to Britain as a manufacturing nation. Charts 1 and 2 show that both motor vehicles, our most important export industry, and the docks are particularly strike-prone.

No strikes statistics give an indication of other forms of industrial action. Bans on overtime by miners and workers

Chart 1

Twenty most stoppage-affected industries:

Stoppages per 100 000 employees (Annual average, 1966–73, UK)

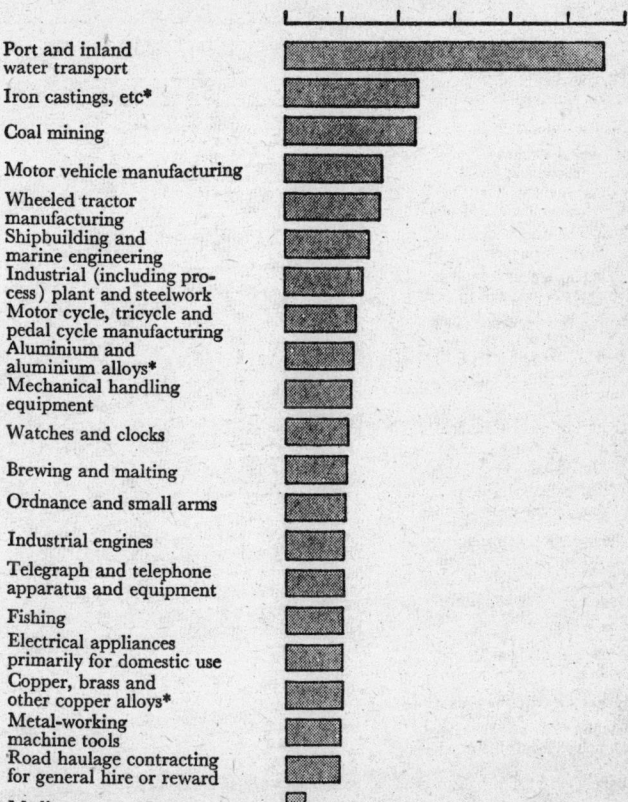

Port and inland water transport

Iron castings, etc*

Coal mining

Motor vehicle manufacturing

Wheeled tractor manufacturing

Shipbuilding and marine engineering

Industrial (including process) plant and steelwork

Motor cycle, tricycle and pedal cycle manufacturing

Aluminium and aluminium alloys*

Mechanical handling equipment

Watches and clocks

Brewing and malting

Ordnance and small arms

Industrial engines

Telegraph and telephone apparatus and equipment

Fishing

Electrical appliances primarily for domestic use

Copper, brass and other copper alloys*

Metal-working machine tools

Road haulage contracting for general hire or reward

Median

*Average based on the three years 1971–73

Source: Department of Employment Gazette, February 1976

Chart 2

Twenty most stoppage-affected industries:

Working days lost per 1000 employees (Annual average, 1966–73, UK)

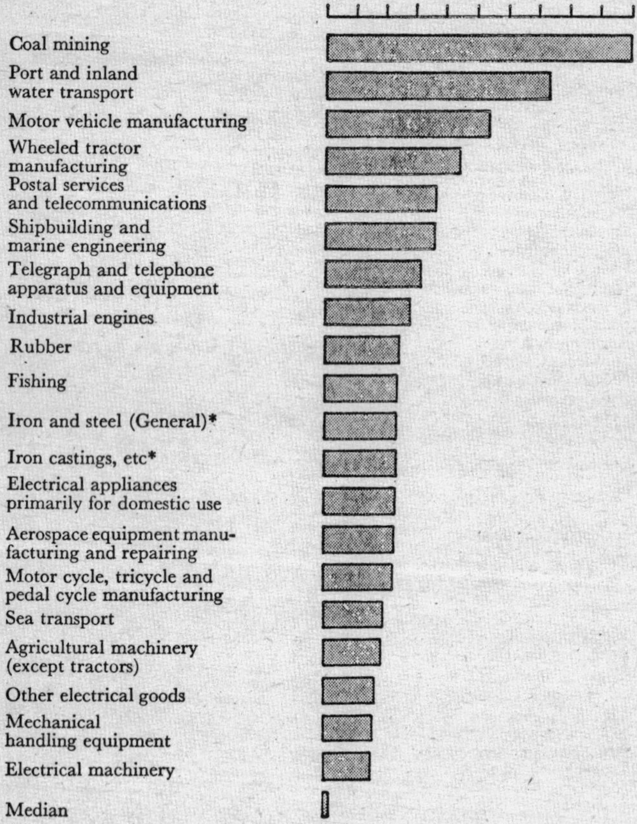

Coal mining	
Port and inland water transport	
Motor vehicle manufacturing	
Wheeled tractor manufacturing	
Postal services and telecommunications	
Shipbuilding and marine engineering	
Telegraph and telephone apparatus and equipment	
Industrial engines	
Rubber	
Fishing	
Iron and steel (General)*	
Iron castings, etc*	
Electrical appliances primarily for domestic use	
Aerospace equipment manufacturing and repairing	
Motor cycle, tricycle and pedal cycle manufacturing	
Sea transport	
Agricultural machinery (except tractors)	
Other electrical goods	
Mechanical handling equipment	
Electrical machinery	
Median	

*Average based on the three years 1971–73

Source: Department of Employment Gazette, February 1976

in electricity supply have in recent years been serious enough to call for government intervention. Working to rule by the three railway unions in 1972 was legally judged to constitute a breach of contract since it prevented the effective running of the railways. There is more to be said about these cases in connection with legal restrictions on strikes, but here we can note that strike statistics do not give the full picture even with regard to overt industrial action.

You may recollect from the chapter on collective bargaining that the total number of strikes or days lost are suspect as indications of the state of labour relations in one firm as compared with another. Constitutional strikes are an integral part of the collective bargaining process. Commercially, there is no doubt that a successful firm may have an apparently 'bad' strike record. Similar considerations apply to nations. Unconstitutional strikes are a different matter. No-one could suggest that they were all part and parcel of collective bargaining. A failure to honour agreements is an obvious indication that something is wrong with labour relations. Since something like 95% of British strikes have been unconstitutional, there is not much point in looking for a nation with a worse record. The evidence here is disputed all the same.

Bad labour relations may not express themselves overtly at all. There are many other indications, such as poor workmanship, absenteeism, bad time-keeping, high labour turnover, and so on. These are not attributable, however, to the manner in which unions and employers negotiate together, at least not entirely. They are certainly not included in strike statistics.

Comparisons with the United States are interesting in this respect. That country has a worse record than Britain in terms of the number of strikes and of days lost. All the same, the heads of two American-based multi-nationals (Ford and Chrysler) have both made scathing comments about the state of British labour relations. In 1972 Henry Ford said, 'There is nothing wrong with Ford of Britain—only with the country . . . We can't recommend any new capital investment in a country constantly dogged with labour problems'. It was only with some difficulty that Chrysler were persuaded by the Government in 1975 to continue their British operations (a substantial loan was part of the persuasion). Presumably it was not just strike statistics that the heads of these companies had in mind. They are both in the motor-vehicle sector, which is not representative of British industry as a whole; but their comments have not helped the Government to encourage overseas investors in Britain.

Arguments about the damage which free collective bargaining does to Britain's economy will continue. Enough has been said to show readers that international comparisons of strike statistics are never likely to be conclusive. In the meantime, the weight of evidence so far as successive governments have been concerned has gone in favour of intervention, even though this may be temporary. In the terms of our original questions, the problem has been seen as economic in its nature, and serious enough to justify government intervention, but the last question about what is to be done has led to further disagreement.

Political implications

Seeing the problem in economic terms is very much in line with the style of British politics ever since the last war. We are in an area where economic and political considerations merge—the area of political economy. It would be foolish to assert that the British problem is entirely economic and to ignore political implications. Incomes policies are intended as a temporary expedient to solve an economic problem, but they have, as will be shown, some important consequences for the practice of democracy.

We have had incomes policies on and off in one form or another ever since the 'sterling crisis' of 1947. There was an agreement on wage restraint between trade unions and the Labour government from 1948 to 1950, although this was in the context of general price controls. A 'price freeze' in 1956–7 restrained incomes as did the 'pay pause' of

1961–2, both of which were introduced by Conservative governments and met with trade union opposition. In December 1964, under another Labour government, there appeared the famous Declaration of Intent, which was signed by the Government, employers' representatives, and the TUC. They were all committed to keeping 'increases in total money incomes in line with increases in real national output'. A fairly sophisticated type of policy was adopted which, at least in its early days, gained much trade union co-operation. Such co-operation waned when it was realised that the 'muscle' of bargaining power was not really compatible with a rational economic argument for a wage increase. The Conservatives were returned in 1970 declaring that incomes policies had been proved a failure. It was, as already noted, their own incomes policy which led to their downfall.

Labour came back in 1974 with assurances that it would uphold the principle of free collective bargaining—a sacrosanct object of the labour movement by now. Within their first year we had the Social Contract (with capitals to distinguish it from a concept known to political theory for a few centuries). As a result of this a flat £6 limit was imposed on wage increases, which was interpreted by the unions as a £6 entitlement and lower-paid workers were quite pleased with the result. The latest development (1976) has been to give tax concessions in return for the TUC's acceptance of wage restraint.

Every incomes policy has come in under a different name, as if there were some anxiety for it not to be associated with those which have gone before. With the possible exception of that following the Declaration of Intent, they were all to be temporary measures 'until we were out of our present difficulties'. The evidence would suggest that our difficulties were chronic rather than temporary.

Politically there are some important consequences when governments so frequently adopt expedient measures against a principle they are supposed to support. The electorate has not seen these policies in election manifestos, and therefore has not voted for an incomes policy at all, much less for a particular type of policy. If there is to be an incomes policy, democratic principles demand that the electorate should have some choice as to its form and content.

Asking the TUC voluntarily to accept wage restraint does not meet this objection. The TUC only represents about half of the nation's workforce, so that the policy can scarcely be said to have been agreed by the other half.

Negotiating cuts in taxes and public expenditure with the TUC, as has happened under the Social Contract, has its apparent absurdities. Putting it crudely, the TUC seems to be doing the government's job in return for allowing the government to look after the TUC's job. Upon pragmatic grounds such arrangements might be justified, but they do not make good constitutional theory. Governments are elected to decide taxes and cuts in public expenditure, not the TUC. Perhaps we should consider what might have happened if Britain's joining the Common Market had been part of such a package deal. Presumably, Britain would have stayed out, although this was against the wishes of the overwhelming majority.

When incomes policies have been adopted, governments have been aware of pressures from Britain's overseas creditors, investors and holders of sterling. As a fact of political economy, they have not been entirely free to form their own opinion. The revenue from North Sea oil is said to offer our salvation. Britain will then, it is alleged, be able to 'pay her way in the world', not have to borrow money from abroad, and sterling will be strong. But if this revenue is to be so important to the national economy, to free collective bargaining, and to our democratic way of life, what then will happen if North Sea oil becomes a strike-prone industry? Are strikes in that industry to be made illegal in the manner of the old Conspiracy and Protection of Property Act? It seems to the writer that free collective bargaining becomes something which Britain is less, not more, able to afford. This point takes us on to consider the way in which modern society is so highly integrated in social as well as economic terms.

Social considerations

Social factors are inter-woven into our economic and political difficulties. Free collective bargaining was conceived in a society which was loosely integrated compared with our own. A strike would not cause anything like the same degree of disruption to other people's lives. Strikes in the gas industry were illegal, as it happens, if they threatened the public supply. Even so, if gas workers were on strike people could light their candles or paraffin lamps; cooking could still be done by an open fire. True, the streets would not be lit, but that presented no great hazards when most traffic moved at the speed of a cart-horse. Compare that situation with what happened in 1972, when workers imposed a ban on overtime (legally permissable, as it would always have been). There was a public outcry. People in all-electric homes lost their lighting, heating and cooking facilities. Those in the upper stories of high-rise flats were trapped because their lifts would not work. The lives of people on kidney-machines were said to be endangered, although the union disputed this. Much of industry, now entirely dependent on a public supply of electricity, was forced onto a three-day week. Perhaps that is a rather extreme contrast, but it serves to illustrate the dependence of modern society upon one group of workers. We leave ourselves with fewer alternatives when any supply or service is cut.

This is more than a problem in economics. We are now questioning the possible damage which a strike may do to the total set of obligations which the participants have to the rest of society. Earlier the morality of strikes was dismissed as irrelevant in the context of collective bargaining. In a total social context the question re-appears. If we can question on moral grounds the effects of strike action upon the 'general public', then we must question whether modern society can afford free collective bargaining. You simply cannot have one without the other. If you still doubt this, think again about the meaning of 'bargaining' and of 'strikes'.

But society in general also has considerable effects upon trade unions in particular. On many counts we live in a highly materialist society. Employers strive through advertisements to sell their goods. Governments pin great faith on economic growth to give the nation a higher standard of living. The present crisis is only seen as a temporary halt in the march to prosperity. Our economy has to be geared to meet rising expectations. There is bound to be an upward pressure on wage costs as workers seek to improve their standard of living. Naturally they want their share of this 'good life' they keep hearing about. That, you may say, is a value judgement. Society has every right to set itself these materialist goals. You are right; but society cannot escape the implications for its industrial relations.

The easy answer is to say that workers must earn their higher living standards and their higher wages through increased productivity. This, you will recollect, was the thinking behind the Declaration of Intent. Unfortunately, it is not quite as easy as that. The very nature of highly industrialised work is such that a worker is not able to affect productivity. There is very little that a worker in the middle of a production line may do to affect output. This, you will remember, was the point of alienation in modern industry, that it took control out of workers' hands. At the other extreme, there are professional people who would find it difficult to show any increase in productivity, such as teachers and doctors. Those who are able to take advantage of this type of policy are a privileged minority.

There are a good many other criticisms that can be made on strictly economic grounds. Generally, one can say that this theory assumes techniques for attributing increases in productivity as between different groups of workers or between labour and capital, which do not exist. Those whose incomes are held down are bound to feel a sense of injustice. This applies especially in a society which finds differentials and relativities so important.

Upon many counts we can see that the whole of society is involved in collective bargaining. This discussion is highly relevant to our first question as to the nature of the problem. With such a high degree of involvement between society in general and trade union activities in particular, we are bound to think in terms of a social problem. If society is at odds with itself, there is not much that the state can do. More than likely the elected government will reflect the same contradictions. But this is to anticipate the subject of the next chapter.

Our problem is a serious one even though it is difficult to be precise as to its nature; evidence in economic terms is disputed, since it has so many political and social implications. We shall be forced to reconsider the nature of the problem in the next chapter after looking at the state's attempts to put things right.

FURTHER READING

This is difficult just because the subject crosses the boundaries of separate disciplines.

Small is Beautiful by E. F. Schumacher (Blond Briggs, 1973) has some interesting criticisms of large plants and highly specialised work as well as of the materialist slant given to society. Otherwise, the best recommendation one can give is to read newspapers critically.

QUESTIONS FOR DISCUSSION

1 Can Britain afford both free collective bargaining and a controlled economy?

2 Recollecting points in the first chapter about the nature of industrial work, do you accept that an industrial society can be anything other than materialist?

Getting it Together Again

Many people, myself included, think the pendulum has swung too far from a belief in *laissez-faire*. Scarcely a problem now arises which is not thought fit for legislation. It was not too surprising when governments of both parties decided to go ahead with extensive intervention in collective bargaining. To be fair it has to be allowed that governments are not schools of philosophy: they cannot afford to contemplate the nature of their problems for ever more. Given a critical situation they are bound to do something, even if only to 'suck it and see'. That they should see the problem in national economic terms is only to be expected, considering their responsibilities.

Neither are their efforts without value, because to some extent they help to reveal the type of problem we have and the limits to what the state can hope to achieve. Nevertheless, there are more general grounds for objecting to state interference with trade unions. One cannot appreciate the hostility which unions show to some proposals without an understanding of these fundamental principles.

In this chapter we shall look at the initial fear felt by trade unions of being sucked into the state apparatus. We shall never know what might have happened if trade unions had been prepared to co-operate with the Labour government's proposals in their 1969 White Paper, 'In Place of Strife' or with the Conservatives' Industrial Relations Act, 1971. That does not mean we do not have a lot to learn from these experiences aside from the degree of hostility they provoked. Previously, unions had co-operated with the National Prices and Income Board, and this has also to be considered. Returning to the root of our problem, the alienating nature of industrial work as we now know it, we can see the importance of more modest contributions from all parties concerned. The responsibilities of society at large are raised in connection with alternative technologies.

There is a well-founded fear that trade unions will disappear inside the state apparatus. This happened both in Italy and Spain. The TUC's break with the communist World Federation and the subsequent founding of the ICFTU are relevant in this context. The extent to which one favours state control is a matter of political opinion. British unions have always, from their origins in pre-democratic society, kept their distance from the state. It may, perhaps, be something of a contradiction that they have favoured more and more state control in other respects. But even those trade unionists who might favour a totalitarian form of society saw the government as trying to hold down wages whilst leaving all other prices free. Government assurances that they were not attacking the independence of trade unions did little to allay fears on that score.

There was a more immediate and practical consideration. A considerable amount of effective power lay in the shop stewards' movement. That, as we have seen, is a highly informal institution and yet one which commands support from rank and file members: it has to from its very nature. A legalistic approach was bound to find fault with the informal system of industrial relations, and at least threaten a valuable institution so far as the shop floor was concerned. Horror at the number of unofficial strikes is not shared by shop stewards and their constituents. When the trade union hierarchy objected to state interference, they had considerable support from the membership.

Government intervention has in fact focused on collective bargaining rather than trade union government or

structure. There is, it is true, provision under the Employment Protection Act to guarantee the independence of
trade unions from employers. But no TUC-affiliated union
has been refused a certificate nor is it likely to be under the
political realities of the Social Contract. Under the Conservative Industrial Relations Act there was a Registrar
of Trade Unions, but the government was only too anxious
for unions to apply for registration. (Technically, they had
to de-register, but that makes no great difference to what is
at issue.) Obviously this approach has a bearing on trade
union government since it affects their primary function.

A difference in emphasis is still important since it indicates
a reluctance to interfere with the internal affairs of trade
unions. There is still a possibility that a future government
will make more stringent regulations for a trade union to
be registered. Conservative spokesmen have mooted a
number of ideas in this direction, the most important being
that national trade union elections must be by postal ballot.
This change of tactic may be justified on the grounds that
since the state does provide trade unions with certain
privileges, it has at least the right to ensure that those
unions are truly representative of their members. Whether
this will again be resented as undue outside interference
remains to be seen.

Recent evidence on attempted reforms of aspects of collective bargaining is not encouraging, although it has to be
considered. The National Board for Prices and Incomes
had a function more extensive than its title might suggest.
This Board issued a number of reports on general topics
such as Productivity Agreements, Payment by Results, and
Job Evaluation. Under an incomes policy they might have
been expected to ensure that wage agreements observed
their recommendations. Their recommendations were,
however, very general. They had no very clear idea as to
how certain reforms were to be brought about. Productivity
agreements were vital to the whole strategy of the Declaration of Intent which had brought the Board into being.
But productivity agreements were suspected of being largely

fictional. Collusion between employers and the trade union concerned was hinted at by the Chairman of the Board, Mr Aubrey Jones, in a remark about the Electrical Contracting Industry. A report of the Board into 'Productivity Agreements in the Road Haulage Industry' did not find that there had in fact been any noticeable increase in productivity. The subsequent demise of the Board arose from their failure to convince the parties concerned or the general public that they were fulfilling a useful function. Some economists, however, still argue that they were successful in restraining growth in incomes.

The Donovan Report led to the establishment in 1969 of the Commission on Industrial Relations. To distinguish it from the above-mentioned Board, the Commission was to deal with procedural rather than substantive matters. Neither body found it possible to observe a strict line of demarcation. The Commission issued a series of reports to do with individual companies, industries and general topics, such as the disclosure of information. The Commission only moved with the consent of all parties concerned. Trade unions, the employers and the government had to agree to a reference being made. It was noticeable that the Commission did not seem to grasp the nettle. The government and the general public had cause to be concerned about the state of industrial relations in, for example, the motor-car industry and Fleet Street, but these were not referred to the Commission. Perhaps this is not surprising in view of the prior agreement that was necessary.

A further difficulty arose from the pragmatic style of the Commission. They had the responsibility to achieve positive results in particular cases having regard to all the factors involved. Their recommendations in particular cases were not, therefore, generally applicable, and indeed were never intended to be. Perhaps, given time, a body of case law would have arisen which would have been of general assistance. Their need, however, to have the co-operation of all parties and therefore to avoid giving offence to individual parties was not calculated to put much bite into their reports. We shall never know because the Commission was never given time. The Conservatives decided to introduce the Industrial Relations Act and this resulted in trade unions withdrawing all co-operation. When Labour returned the Commission was quietly buried (1974), although its advisory function was transferred to ACAS.

The Conservatives were not the first to suggest that the state might intervene more directly in collective bargaining. In 1969 the Labour government issued its White Paper, 'In Place of Strife'. It was in fact this White Paper which accepted Donovan's recommendation that there should be a Commission on Industrial Relations, but it went much further in giving the Secretary of State powers to prevent or at least hold up strikes. It was these powers which provoked the hostility of the trade union movement. As a final resort, the Secretary of State had in certain circumstances the power to order strikers back to work for a period of twenty-eight days—'the conciliation pause'. It was also proposed that serious strikes, those affecting the national economy, could be held up whilst a ballot was conducted to ensure that the majority of members were in favour of strike action. The first proposal was aimed at cutting the number of unconstitutional and unofficial strikes, which the government saw as the chief disorder. The second had a more general aim to protect the economy.

In the uproar which ensued great stress was laid on the 'penal sanctions' with which the government proposed to enforce these measures. It is very difficult to be precise as to the reasons behind the trade unions' antagonism to these proposals. Only a minority were prepared to discuss them in detail, and a special conference simply rejected the whole package. The government drafted a milder bill but they lost an intervening election in 1970. Since these proposals were never debated in detail, one can only draw the general conclusion of intense trade union opposition to state intervention.

The Industrial Relations Act (1971) which the Conservatives subsequently introduced was imbued with the idea that industrial relations should be subject to the rule of law. Collective agreements were to be legally binding. A registrar would vet union rules and have powers to strike unions off the register. Shop stewards' duties were, therefore, to be clearly specified in rule books. The Act also sought to put an end to pre-entry closed shops on the grounds that an individual should have the right *not* to belong to a trade union. Sympathetic strike actions were virtually outlawed on rather legalistic grounds, the contract of employment being the essential document and this did not concern outside parties. Other proposals were similar to those of 'In Place of Strife' including provisions for 'cooling off periods' and ballots, though in a much wider range of circumstances.

Since the union movement had already defeated the Labour Party's proposals, they were not likely to welcome these more restrictive measures. But the government pinned its faith on the British being a law-abiding people. What followed proved that without doing anything illegal, a determined movement could render the law impotent. Experience also showed that within the informal system, some workers in strategically important industries were in fact prepared to break the law.

Since the TUC ordered all its members to de-register, it was obvious that the movement was prepared to forego its legal privileges rather than submit to what it regarded as an unwarranted degree of interference. They were not thereby breaking the law, but it put the government into overt confrontation with nearly the whole trade union movement, which was an impossible situation. Without breaking their contracts of employment, workers in electricity and coal showed that they could inflict considerable damage on their employers—the government as it so happens—and on the national economy. Bans on overtime were quite lawful, but no less serious on that account. When the three railway unions imposed a work to rule, it was finally judged to be illegal. But it made strange reading to learn that a worker who obeyed his contract to the letter was at the same time breaking that contract. Closed shops were 'unlawful', meaning that they could not be defended in court; they were not 'illegal', in that parties to them could not be prosecuted for no other reason than that. Closed shops were effectively maintained even in government establishments, and the whole situation became somewhat farcical. Long and damaging strikes in the motor-vehicle industry resulted from individuals who asserted their right not to belong to a union.

With the notable exception of the AUEW, unions as official institutions were not prepared to break the law. Given our informal system, that meant little. To be more precise, the Industrial Relations Court could bring considerable pressure to bear on trade unions, even to the extent of confiscating their funds. But when it came to dealing with shop stewards there was a completely different problem. During the long dispute about loading containers (1971–72) it was quite clear that some shop stewards from the docks were happier to be in prison than the government were to have them there. It was in fact a hitherto rather obscure government official who secured their release. The strike at a cold storage depot involved two groups of men from the *same* union, the Transport and General Workers. How then could legal sanctions against the union do any good? The rule of law is not appropriate to all circumstances, and if it is to be applied in circumstances where it cannot be enforced, the law itself tends to fall into disrepute. That is in fact an apt summary of this whole episode.

At the outset it was said that recent evidence on state intervention was not very encouraging. We do have some impressive evidence, however, as to what may or not be achieved through legal enactment. Prospects are not good. We are obliged to look in other directions, and that may be no bad thing. Laws are only a superstructure based upon certain economic and social realities. Industrial relations as we know them attempt to reconcile the differences which arise from a certain method of production. If industrial relations seem to be breaking down, perhaps instead of going to a higher level of authority we should go back to the root of our problems, to the alienating nature of industrial work.

Within the limits of existing technology there is a great deal that can be done to humanise industrial work and we shall be looking at a number of interesting job enrichment schemes throughout Europe. Some firms have made a radical re-appraisal of their organisations and the results look promising.

Technology does impose limits on what can be done to make work more satisfying. In recent years man's subjection to technology has been fiercely contested. Since alternative technologies carry implications for the whole of society, if we are to make any progress in this direction it is essential that there should be an integrated approach. At present this type of thinking is largely speculative, but it does open our minds to exciting possibilities for the future.

Job enrichment

A Work Research Unit has been set up within the Department of Employment. The unit is staffed by behavioural scientists, engineers and industrial relations experts. It will provide information and advice on reducing the humdrum element in work by job re-design and other changes in work organisation. If required it will help firms to plan and carry out projects. The unit is keen that unions and managers should jointly explore possibilities of making work more satisfying. A series of projects in research institutes will be financed from a government grant.

Representatives of the TUC, alongside those from Government and the CBI were on a steering group which set up this unit. Unions in other countries have perhaps demonstrated their interest in a more militant manner. Workers at the Renault factory in Paris walked out in March 1972, not for more pay but in protest at the monotony of their work. The United Auto Workers Union of America are demanding changes in the assembly line, which they regard as a most dehumanising way to work.

A signpost for the future arises from our previous discussion of participation. There are possibilities of a new relationship between labour and capital. More control over the aims of industry by workers could radically alter working conditions. As was stressed in the section on participation, it is important for worker directors to accept the value judgements on which policy is based. A major question is whether the profit motive is to remain pre-eminent or whether it can co-exist with a drive for a finer quality of working life. If employers are prepared to accept something like the Norwegian system, whereby the annual general meeting of shareholders is not able to veto a decision taken by the board, then the TUC would be more optimistic about the future of industrial relations.

Management's new participatory style also points away from alienation. Along this road we can see that management will have to be increasingly educated to deal with people and not merely trained to manipulate labour. There will be little progress towards the integration of work and the worker unless certain management specialists are prepared to look again at some of their assumptions. Method study can be applied to the reduction of alienation, provided that work study engineers are not trained simply to increase production: problems not directly connected with production cannot be hived off to a catch-all category known as 'personnel management'. If line management were better educated at their job, many of the psychological wounds at present inflicted need never happen. There would be no need for a personnel department to act as a kind of first-aid post for injured egos.

At present professional institutions perceive the necessity for such education, although they vary in the extent to which they have thought through the implications for their whole practice. A general tendency is to put the odd paper on industrial relations into the syllabus, without questioning the bearing which it has on all their other subjects. If teachers cannot see any connection there is no good reason to expect their students to do so. Industrial relations, sociology, psychology and economics will all be left in separate compartments of a student's mind, and quite unrelated to his main studies as an engineer or accountant or whatever. The results of studying social science subjects ought to be more evident across the spectrum of managerial tuition.

There is a growing body of evidence as to what can be achieved by enlightened management. Philips at Eindhoven in 1969 experimented with charging seven people to assemble a black and white television set. Previously over thirty workers had been involved, each with a more minute task. At Norsk-Hydro, the Norwegian conglomerate, workers in its fertiliser factories are organised into autonomous teams. Each team allocates various tasks which have to be done among themselves. Job rotation occurs and teams have also taken over specialist functions such as quality control. The results here are said to be quite spectacular; employees are much more enthusiastic about their work. Olivetti, the Italian business-machine manufacturers, let team captains decide on work schedules and quality control. Their supervisory service has been given a research and advisory function. In 1972 Saab-Scania set up a new factory at Sodertalje for assembling car engines. An overhead cable carries work to teams of four. Once again each team is allowed to allocate tasks as they see fit. This method has been proved to be almost as fast as that of a conventional assembly line. ICI abolished clocking-in at their Gloucester factory, and then, in 1968, revised their production line to create a better working environment. Workers were given much more responsibility and supervisors became advisory staff. This venture was studied by a group of sociologists from Bath University who reported in a book called *The Nylon Spinners*. Although about 80% of workers appreciated improvements, they still described their work as monotonous.[1] A French sociologist, Yves Delamotte, has commented

---

[1] See pp. 136-7, *The Nylon Spinners* by S. Cotgrove and others (Allen & Unwin, 1971).

that the scope for job enrichment is limited by the 'constraints of technology'.

'Alternative' or 'intermediate' technology is still in its infancy, though it is rapidly attracting more attention in Britain, North America, Sweden and France. Two prominent organisations are the Intermediate Technology Development Group in Britain and the Brace Research Institute in Canada. Both are engaged in exploring labour-intensive methods of production using local materials, mainly for the benefit of developing countries. E. F. Schumacher, the father of intermediate technology, sees the value of this work for advanced countries. Amongst other reasons he gives the present damage to humanity under typical industrial conditions. There has in fact been quite a considerable spin off as more people in advanced countries, particularly the young, see the relevance of this type of research to our acute problems of alienation.

Ivan Illich has coined the phrase 'convivial technology'. His idea is that 'tools', by which he means all rationally designed devices, are intrinsic to social relationships, and therefore should be designed to enhance our range of freedom. There is a lot of thinking on similar lines. Some see advanced electronics as opening up great possibilities for decentralisation, which would enable local communities to control industry better and thus make the whole system more democratic. The technical point is that an electronically controlled machine can perform a wide range of functions, so that there is less need for factories to specialise: an exactly opposite trend to that of division of labour.

This might all seem highly speculative, not to say quaint, were it not for one peculiar feature of our present stage of development: if we want anything badly enough we tend to get it. When the Americans decided to land on the moon, who doubted that they would do it? The question is not so much whether a thing can be done as whether it is worth doing. There is some evidence of what can be done; there would be more if society were fully determined to humanise industrial work. Technology helps to determine the type of society we live in, but society can if it so desires shape technology.

Alternative technology ought not to be confused with primitive technology. Primitive societies are restricted in choice by their ignorance and poverty. There is no excuse for rich, advanced countries. If they allege that technological imperatives leave them no choice, they pretend to be more primitive than they are.

Perhaps the most radical experiment carried out so far is in the Volvo works at Kalmar. There the assembly line concept has been completely abandoned. Teams of 15 to 25 men are given a fairly substantial and meaningful task, say the completion of a car's entire electrical system. Completed work is then fed into bays, from where it is drawn by other teams of workers. This is a more expensive method of production. For such technology to become widespread, society would have to opt for a better working life and have rather fewer material goods. If we simply measure the standard of living in material terms then there would possibly be a reduction. More people are coming to think that less materialism would improve the *quality* of our lives. Advocates of alternative technology would go much further than Volvo have done: a high degree of personal mobility as provided by motor-cars is a social objective which they would question severely. Certainly a change in society's demands would do more to alter technology than could ever be achieved by job enrichment schemes.

Our generation is fortunate in that it has better opportunities to resume control of industry than any previously. Industry can be made to serve society; machines be made to serve people instead of the other way round. If these opportunities are grasped, then the whole ground of industrial relations will be altered. That would indicate that we were living in the 'post industrial age' and the long industrial revolution would finally be over.

FURTHER READING

News from Nowhere by William Morris (Routledge, 1970)

Man-Made Futures edited by Nigel Cross and others
(Hutchinson, 1974)

QUESTIONS FOR DISCUSSION

1   Given your ideal society, what if any would be the
differences between leisure and work?
2   What inventions would society have been better off
without and what would you like to see invented?
3   Do you see trade unions as being progressive or
reactionary in the face of technological change? Will
they defend their members' existing jobs and differentials
or will they welcome a liberation from industrial work?
4   Does Britain's dependence on exports mean that she
is in no position to opt for alternative technology?

Glossary

There are a number of terms which, although in everyday use, carry a special meaning in industrial relations. In the explanations that follow some key concepts have been taken in pairs, as one helps to explain the other. Indeed the difference between two terms is often crucial to a proper understanding of the British system of industrial relations.

Alienation: literally, an estrangement or transfer of ownership. In industrial relations it can simply refer to the fact that tools and machines are owned by employers instead of workers. More generally it refers to the loss of control over their work by employees, with a consequent lack of interest.

Arbitration and conciliation: an arbitrator is a judge whose verdict or decision must be accepted by both sides. It is of the essence of arbitration in free collective bargaining that both sides agree to go to arbitration rather than solve the dispute through industrial action.

A conciliator merely brings the two sides together and helps them to resolve their differences. He does *not* impose a binding decision. An analogy often given is that an arbitrator may be compared to a divorce-court judge and a conciliator to a marriage guidance counsellor.

Bargaining agent: the institution, usually a trade union, which is recognised by employers for collective bargaining purposes.

Blacking: a form of industrial action whereby workers refuse to do certain work—maybe to operate a particular machine or to handle some product.

Code of practice: not exclusive to industrial relations—the Highway Code is, perhaps, the best known. There are many others in the health and safety field. A code of practice is a document prepared by a government department or agency to give general advice. Anyone who does not follow a code to the letter is not necessarily breaking the law. But failure to observe such a code would provide strong evidence of some form of neglect if produced in court.

Closed shop: a workplace where all workers must belong to an appropriate union. A *pre-entry* closed shop requires all prospective employees to be members of an appropriate union. A *post-entry* closed shop allows employees a probationary period during which they must join the union if they are not members already.

Collective agreement: the document which sets out all that has been agreed in areas of joint control. Although signed by both sides, in Britain it is not legally binding unless both sides have agreed that it should be so.

Collective bargaining: the process whereby workers deal with their employers as a group rather than as individuals. Originally, there was a cash bargain, in the sense that a specific wage was paid for a certain quality and amount of work under certain conditions. Nowadays the term is used much more loosely to describe any negotiations between employers and trade unions. Many of the agreements arrived at fall outside the law of contract.

Conciliation: see *arbitration.*

Confederation: a working arrangement between various unions in an industry. Individual trade union rule books remain paramount.

Constitutional and official strikes: an official strike is one called by the proper authority under union rules—usually the executive council. Most strikes in Britain begin by being unofficial, since they are called by shop stewards who do not have that power according to the rule book. If they last long enough to come to the attention of executive councils, they are then accepted or rejected. If they are supported by the executive council, they become official.

A constitutional strike is one taken after the agreed procedure has been exhausted. An unconstitutional strike is in breach of such an agreement. It follows that a strike may be official and yet unconstitutional.

Consultation and negotiation: consultation takes place over those matters which are still subject to managerial prerogative. Having taken the opinions of their workers, management are still entirely responsible for their subsequent decision.

Negotiation takes place over matters which are subject to joint control. Usually an agreement will be drawn up and signed by both sides, indicating their joint responsibility for its maintenance.

Craft Unions: strictly speaking, a union exclusively for craftsmen in a single trade; it must now be extended to cover unions recruiting in a number of crafts. There are other unions which are still craft-dominated, that is, still following the craft traditions even though they have amended their rules to allow unskilled or semi-skilled workers into membership (the AUEW is one example).

Differentials and relativities: differences in pay between grades, say skilled and unskilled, are known as differentials.

Differences in pay between groups, each of which covers a number of grades, are known as relativities. For example, the wages of all workers in the mining industry may be compared with those of workers in the motor-car industry.

Division of labour: an economic term to describe the division of a task or job into a number of relatively simple operations. Historically, the need for craftsmen was thus largely dispensed with and the introduction of machinery facilitated. In the process, however, new skills are created as complicated machinery has to be manufactured and maintained. For the bulk of workers division of labour remains the chief source of the alienation of their work.

Economies of scale: Those economies or savings which result from large-scale production.

Employers' associations or federations: a combination of employers to deal with matters of mutual interest. They do not always deal with industrial relations.

Formal and informal systems of collective bargaining: The definitive feature of the formal system is that union representatives are acting within their powers as set out by union rules. The present formal system is that between full-time officials and employers. 'Donovan' described the national agreement as the keystone of this system.

The informal system is commonly that based on negotiations between management and shop stewards within a plant. 'Informal' is the appropriate work because the power of shop stewards to negotiate lies mainly outside union rule books.

Free collective bargaining: means 'free from government intervention or control'—also referred to as *Voluntary* collective bargaining.

General Union: a trade union which is open to all grades and skills in any industry. In fact this type of union is most successful in recruiting unskilled or semi-skilled in areas of new technology.

Ideological and instrumental trade unionism: the effort to maintain a degree of control over working practices is a direct challenge to increasing alienation, and is referred to as ideological trade unionism. It is more associated with craft than with general unions.

Instrumental trade unionism accepts increased alienation provided there is sufficient financial reward. It concentrates on a better wage bargain in strictly materialist terms.

Industrial Unions: these are open to all grades within a single industry. The National Union of Mineworkers, for example, recruits all grades in the coal-mining industry.

Instrumental trade unionism: see *ideological trade unionism.*

Joint control: control by both unions and employers. Wages are commonly subject to joint control.

Managerial prerogative: the right of management to make certain decisions without having to obtain the agreement of trade unions. Obviously this operates outside the area of joint control.

Negotiation: see *consultation.*

Official strikes: see *constitutional strikes.*

Participation: in current usage refers to the election of workers' representatives to boards of directors or parallel bodies in the public sector.

Picketing: standing outside an employer's premises to enlist support for industrial action.

Procedural and substantive agreements: procedural agreements lay down the steps to be followed in settlement of a dispute. For example, the first step for an individual with a grievance may be for that person to take it up with his supervisor.

Substantive agreements deal with the wage bargain. On

one side is the contribution to be made by labour (hours of work, etc.) and on the other side of the bargain is labour's reward, including not only pay but fringe benefits such as pensions.

Both types of agreement may form part of the same document.

Producer co-operative: a workshop or factory governed by its workers.

Recognition: a union is 'recognised' when it is accepted by employers as a bargaining agent.

Relativities: see *differentials.*

Status quo clause: one that lays down that there shall be no alteration to working arrangements if the union disputes the right of management to make such an alteration without their prior agreement. Such clauses become effective when there is some doubt about the area of managerial prerogative.

Strike: a withdrawal of labour by a group of employees.

Structure of trade unions: the distribution of workers between different unions. For example, the proportion of workers in general unions is a question of trade union structure. It does *not* refer to the administrative organisation of a union.

Substantive agreement: see *procedural agreement.*

Syndicalism: trade unionism directed at revolutionary change through industrial action. It contrasts with the collective bargaining tradition which leaves fundamental changes in society to the political wing of the Labour movement.

White-collar trade union: a union exclusively for white-collar workers of one or more categories.

Work to rule: a form of industrial action. By the strictest interpretation of working rules, trade unions seek to hinder production and thus bring pressure to bear on employers.

Abbreviations used in the Text

ACAS—Advisory, Arbitration and Conciliation Service
ASTMS—Association of Scientific, Technical and
  Managerial Staffs
AUEW—Amalgamated Union of Engineering Workers
CAC—Central Arbitration Committee
CBI—Confederation of British Industry
CIR—Commission on Industrial Relations
CPSA—Civil and Public Services Association
CSEU—Confederation of Shipbuilding and
  Engineering Unions
EETU/PTU—Electrical, Electronic, Telecommunications
  and Plumbing Trade Union
ETUC—European Trade Union Confederation
FTO—Full-time Official of trade union
GMWU—General and Municipal Workers' Union
ICFTU—International Confederation of Free Trade
  Unions
ILO—International Labour Organisation
JIB—Joint Industry Board
JIC—Joint Industry Council
JSSC—Joint Shop Stewards' Committee
NALGO—National and Local Government
  Officers Association
NUM—National Union of Mineworkers
NUPE—National Union of Public Employees
NUR—National Union of Railwaymen
NUT—National Union of Teachers

PBR—Payment by results
SOGAT—Society of Graphical and Allied Trades
TGWU—Transport and General Workers Union
TUC—Trades Union Congress
UCATT—Union of Construction, Allied Trades and
  Technicians
UPOW—Union of Post Office Workers
USDAW—Union of Shop, Distributive and Allied
  Workers
WCL—World Confederation of Labour
WFTU—World Federation of Trade Unions

Acts of Parliament relevant to the Text

1799–1800	'The Combination Acts'
1823	Master and Servant Act
1824–5	Combination Laws Repeal Acts
1831–1960	The Truck Acts
1832	First Reform Act
1867	Master and Servant Act
1867	Second Reform Act
1871	Trade Union Act
1875	Conspiracy and Protection of Property Act
1876	Trade Union Amendment Act
1896	Conciliation Act
1906	Trade Disputes Act
1909	Trade Boards Act
1913	Trade Union Act
1919	Industrial Courts Act
1919	Police Act
1920	Emergency Powers Act
1933 and 1963	Children and Young Persons Act
1944	Education Act
1953	The Post Office Act
1959	Wages Councils Act
1959	Terms and Conditions of Employment Act
1963	Disabled Persons Act
1964	Trade Union (Amalgamations, etc.) Act
1965	Redundancy Payments Act
1968	Race Relations Act

1970 Equal Pay Act
1972 Contracts of Employment Act
1974 Health and Safety at Work, etc. Act
1974 Trade Union and Labour Relations Act
1975 Employment Protection Act
1975 Sex Discrimination Act
1976 Trade Union and Labour Relations
     (Amendment) Act

Examination Questions

The following questions have been taken with the permission of the institutes mentioned from their past examination papers. They have been arranged as they appear to fit the three major parts of this book.

Part 1

Describe the main stages in the development of the present trades union structure.

Institute of Practitioners in
Work Study, Organisation and Methods;
November 1975, Examination in
Behavioural Science and Personnel Function

How would you account for the diversity of size and type of trade unions in Britain at the present time?

Institute of Personnel Management;
June 1976, Part 2 Examination

Examine the part played by ideology in trade union behaviour.

Institute of Works Managers;
Summer 1973, External Examination
Industrial Relations Part 1

What indicates 'success' for a trade union?

Institute of Personnel Management;
June 1976, Part 2 Examination

'The shop steward is essential to the union, needed by workers, necessary to management yet a danger to all of them!' Explain the situation. What can a works manager do about such a dilemma?

Institute of Works Managers;
Summer 1973, External Examination
Industrial Relations Part 1

Part 2

What is meant by 'management prerogatives' and by 'trade union rights' in the context of a collective agreement? How useful do you think it is to spell these out in a collective agreement?

Institute of Personnel Management;
November 1975, Part 2 Examination

To what extent does collective bargaining in this country concern itself with *both* a fair day's work *and* a fair day's pay?

Institute of Personnel Management;
November 1976, Part 3 Examination

From the point of view of a student of Industrial Relations what factors need to be taken into account when seeking to interpret the statistics of industrial conflict?

Institution of Works Managers;
Summer 1976, Part 1 Certificate in
Industrial Relations

To what extent, in which circumstances, and by what means, does the law uphold the trade unionist's right to strike?

Institute of Personnel Management;
November 1976, Part 3 Examination

In respect of which individual terms and conditions of employment has legislation imposed a minimum or standard? Could you offer an explanation of why these have been

treated in this way, whilst others are left for determination
by the contracting parties themselves?

Institute of Personnel Management;
November 1976, Part 2 Examination

There is currently considerable discussion of 'participation'
in industry. How far would you regard this as a product of
trade union ideology, and how far a product of management
ideology?

Institute of Personnel Management;
November 1976, Part 3 Examination

Part 3

Discuss how, and why, the power and authority of employers
and unions have changed in recent years.

Institute of Practitioners in
Work Study, Organisation and Methods;
June 1976, Examination in
Behavioural Science and Personnel Function.

Our pattern of industrial relations has been described as a
'voluntary system'. What characteristics can be asserted to
be necessary to the maintenance of the system as a 'voluntary'
one?

Institute of Personnel Management;
November 1976, Part 2 Examination

How far can the increasing incidence of 'work-ins', workers'
control, etc., be seen as an expression of syndicalism?

Institution of Works Managers;
Summer 1976, Part 1 Certificate in
Industrial Relations

Index

PUBLIC RELATIONS

HERBERT LLOYD

In today's complex world, mutual understanding between any organisation and its respective public is essential. The deliberate and sustained effort to establish and maintain this empathy is given the title Public Relations.

Herbert Lloyd is a widely recognised authority on the subject of Public Relations and gives here a lucid and invaluable introduction to his chosen field. It is now possible to understand the basic principles involved and to develop the rudimentary techniques of dealing with the problems that arise when promoting good relations.

The information and practice which this volume offer highlight the basic qualities needed in a competent Public Relations practitioner and provide valuable information – including relevant examination questions – for any students of business studies.

TEACH YOURSELF BOOKS

OFFICE MANAGEMENT

P. W. BETTS

The role of the office manager has completely changed in recent years, but the critical part he plays in determining the success of a concern still remains often unrecognised.

The on going business is dependent upon successful administrative operations at all organisation levels. Hence the generation of more and more paperwork and the ever increasing demand for administrative staff, but more paper and staff are not necessarily the answer. In this book the author gives a lucid account of the information and techniques essential to the departmental office manager. The text offers the business student an overall account of administrative management and explains the need for increased expertise in this practice. Executives responsible for organisational structure will also find this book invaluable.

An invaluable text for students of management studies and in particular for students of the Diploma in Administrative Management, the Certificate in Office Supervision and of the Final Examinations of the Institute of Chartered Secretaries and Administrators, the Institute of Cost and Management Accountants and the Association of Certified Accountants.

TEACH YOURSELF BOOKS

PERSONNEL MANAGEMENT

RON CURSON

Personnel management is concerned with people in all fields of employment and their relationships within an enterprise.

This book links together the different aspects of personnel management. These are examined not only from the standpoint of the specialist but also to reflect the needs and responsibilities of all managers in their dealings with people.

The theme is developed in a practical way commencing with the involvement of all the functional areas of management in determining the organisation's corporate strategy and then progressing through the stages of development and implementation of effective manpower plans, training, work patterns, safety, appraisal and industrial relations. The ways in which current practices have developed are outlined and the effects of legislation discussed.

Ron Curson is principal lecturer in Human Resources at Birklands Management Centre of the Hatfield Polytechnic.

TEACH YOURSELF BOOKS

MARKETING

JOHN STAPLETON

One of the better definitions of marketing is that—
'Marketing is the management process which identifies,
anticipates and supplies customer requirements efficiently
and profitably'. This is not new as a basic concept but what
is new is the development of modern sophisticated
techniques being increasingly introduced into the different areas of marketing.

In this book, John Stapleton examines these techniques
in turn and demonstrates how they act together as
components of the total marketing activity. By verbalising
the concepts of marketing and by clarifying the reasoning
behind marketing practice, the author provides an analysis
of these marketing components, their function and
relevance.

The book also provides a basic but wide description
of marketing activity, with individual chapters covering
specific areas such as marketing research, product planning
and pricing, marketing planning, distribution and selling,
and the sales force. Professional narketing men will find
here a valuable source of information and stimulus, while
students of the Insitute of Marketing's Qualifying
Certificate and Diploma courses will find this book an
ideal introductory text.

TEACH YOURSELF BOOKS